THINKING ABOUT THE PROPHETS

University of Nebraska Press
Lincoln

Thinking about the Prophets

A Philosopher Reads the Bible

KENNETH SEESKIN

The Jewish Publication Society
Philadelphia

All rights reserved. Published by the University of
Nebraska Press as a Jewish Publication Society book.
Manufactured in the United States of America.

Library of Congress Cataloging-in-Publication Data
Names: Seeskin, Kenneth, 1947– author.
Title: Thinking about the prophets: a philosopher reads
the Bible / Kenneth Seeskin, The Jewish Publication
Society, Philadelphia.
Description: Lincoln: University of Nebraska Press,
2020. | Series: JPS essential Judaism | Includes
bibliographical references.
Identifiers: LCCN 2020004127
ISBN 9780827615052 (paperback)
ISBN 9780827618527 (epub)
ISBN 9780827618534 (mobi)
ISBN 9780827618541 (pdf)
Subjects: LCSH: Bible. Prophets—Criticism,
interpretation, etc. | Bible. Job—Criticism,
interpretation, etc. | Bible. Prophets—Influence. |
Bible. Job—Influence. | Spiritual life—Judaism. |
Spiritual life—Christianity.
Classification: LCC BS1286 .S44 2020 |
DDC 224/.06—dc23
LC record available at https://lccn.loc.gov/2020004127

Set in Merope by Mikala R. Kolander.

To the memory of Sherry Wasserman

Contents

Acknowledgments

Like *Thinking about the Torah*, this book is the result of years of teaching, studying, and writing on questions raised by the Hebrew Bible. I acknowledge the support of friends and colleagues who have helped shaped my thinking. In no particular order, they include Michael Morgan, Adriano Fabris, Menachem Kellner, Regina Schwartz, Lenn Goodman, Barry Wimpfheimer, Steven Nadler, Joseph Edelheit, David Novak, Martin Kavka, Haim Kreisel, David Shatz, Roslyn Weiss, Josef Stern, Charles Manekin, Benjamin Sommer, James Diamond, Alan Mittleman, Laurie Zoloth, Gary Saul Morson, Stefano Perfetti, and Leora Batnitzky. Special thanks are due to my friend and former colleague Mira Balberg, for lengthy discussions and detailed comments on every aspect of this book.

I also wish to thank Rabbi Barry Schwartz, director of The Jewish Publication Society (JPS), and Joy Weinberg, the JPS managing editor, for valuable editorial assistance. It is rare in this day and age for an author to get sentence-by-sentence feedback on his or her work, but that is exactly what The Jewish Publication Society offered me, and I am extremely grateful. I am also grateful to the University of Nebraska Press, publishing partner of JPS, for providing an attractive venue for authors like me. Finally, I want to thank Benjamin Ricciardi for research assistance.

All quotations from the Hebrew Bible are taken from the NJPS (New Jewish Publication Society) translation of 1985 unless otherwise noted. All Talmudic citations are from the Babylonian Talmud unless otherwise indicated by the letter "Y" for the Jerusalem Talmud.

Preface

Children of Prophets

Thinking about the Prophets: A Philosopher Reads the Bible looks at the great literary prophets whose ministry ran from the eighth to the sixth centuries BCE: Amos, Hosea, First Isaiah, Jeremiah, Ezekiel, Second Isaiah, and Job. Their teachings occupy a pivotal position in the history of both Judaism and Christianity and constitute one of the great achievements of the human spirit.

Important as these messages are, however, they are not always easy to stomach, and in this day and age, they are often forgotten. Within the synagogue on Sabbath and festival days, discussions typically focus on the Torah portion. Short passages from the prophets are relegated to the haftarah and, in my experience, rarely discussed in detail, if discussed at all. Meanwhile, in churches, the prophets are read mainly as forerunners to Jesus. In short, the books of the prophets are rarely read in full.

For some modern readers, the message of the prophets is too controversial to put before a public audience. As the twentieth-century theologian Abraham Joshua Heschel remarked, they are some of the most disturbing people who ever lived. Many passages portend doom. Others are critical of existing religious practices. Thus Amos 5:21–22:

I loathe, I spurn your festivals,
I am not appeased by your solemn assemblies.
If you offer Me burnt offerings—or your meal offerings—

xi

I will not accept them;
I will pay no heed

In a nutshell, Amos is telling us that the religion his contemporaries practiced was a sham.

Might God be just as disdainful of our festivals and assemblies today? The modern biblical scholar Marc Brettler asks how we would respond to someone who stood up in public and said:

Thus said the Lord. / For three transgressions of the residents of Manhattan. / For Four, I will not revoke it: / Because they shop in expensive shops and neglect the poor, / Eat in five-star restaurants while others starve. / I will send down fire upon Fifth Avenue, / A conflagration on 57th St. / And it shall devour the fancy penthouses, /Destroy the mansions. / And the people of "the city" shall be exiled to California — said the Lord.[1]

Seen in this light, Amos and the other prophets pose a serious threat to our current ways of doing things. Not surprisingly, today's religious leaders typically water down the prophets' messages, read them in a perfunctory manner, or do not read them at all. And yet, to Amos's point, I argue in the pages that follow that neither he nor the rest of the prophets wanted the people to relinquish their festivals and assemblies altogether. Rather, they wanted people to ask whether their festivals and assemblies fulfill the purpose for which they were intended. Do they enhance moral or religious sensitivity? Do they help us to follow in the ways of God, which means (among other things) to insist on justice and protect the poor?

What is true of Amos is also true of those who followed in his footsteps: They challenged existing authority and established new ways of thinking. Hosea accused the people of breaking the promise they made to God. First Isaiah agreed with Amos that God despised the people's festivals, and went on to tell a king facing invasion by a foreign power to trust in God rather than horses and chariots. Jeremiah mocked the secular and religious leadership of his day and warned the people that taking refuge in the Temple would not help them. His near contemporary Ezekiel said that in God's eyes, the sins of Israel are even worse than those of its neighbors—so much so that when punishment is inflicted, parents will eat the flesh of their children and children will eat the flesh of their parents.

In my view, we do these people an injustice if we diminish the shock value of their messages. Broadly speaking, the prophets present us with a deep and abiding question: What does it mean to serve God? Is it enough to perform the required rituals, or must we ask what effect these rituals have on the people who perform them and the society of which they are a part?

To answer this question, we must ask how to balance a well-established religious tradition with the need to make changes or modifications. The rituals mandated by Jewish Law have stood the test of time and kept the people together despite two millennia without a homeland or a central place of worship. It would be foolish to drop them in favor of a trendy alternative. By the same token, it would be foolish to ignore the question of whether those in charge of existing institutions have drowned out dissident voices to the point where the institutions no longer fulfill their original purpose. Admittedly, change can be disruptive, both to the institution and to the lives of those who serve it. Nonetheless, successful institutions find a way to embrace change by taking criticism seriously and not just tolerating but finding a place for dissident voices.

Although the prophets maintained that they were taking Judaism back to its core values, and some of them came from established priestly families, it is undeniable that they served as divinely authorized whistle-blowers. Kings, priests, other prophets, judges, merchants—in short almost everyone in a position of authority—were targets for their criticism. How are we to consider these whistle-blowers in our own era? We can treat the prophets in a purely ceremonial fashion, admiring their rhetoric and assigning them space in a worship service. But if this is all we do, we sell them short. To take them seriously, we have to ask whether the religion we ourselves practice can answer the challenges they voiced. Do our prayers motivate us to stand up for the rights of the poor, the sick, and the abused? Are we serving God each and every day with purity of intention and action? Are we sincere when we ask God for forgiveness? These are just some of the questions the prophets force us to ask.

The standard Jewish position is that prophecy came to an end with the destruction of the Second Temple, if not some time before. Even if this is true, it does not follow that the voice of the prophets can no longer be heard. As I see it, Hillel was surely right when he said that if we are not prophets, then we are nonetheless children of prophets (*Pesaḥim* 66b). As children of prophets, we can do no better than to listen to the voice of our ancestors.

In This Book

This book attempts to do right by the prophets by looking at their writings and asking how they influenced later thinkers. Despite the long years that separate us from them, their lessons are as telling for us as they were for our ancestors. Indeed, the timeless nature of their message is part of what justifies their claim to speak for God.

The chapters take up the prophets Amos, Hosea, First Isaiah, Jeremiah, Ezekiel, Second Isaiah, and Job in chronological order, set a historical context for their teachings, and examine their teachings in light of later thinkers and historical developments. Amos raises questions about the nature of moral reasoning, Hosea about the divine persona, First Isaiah about divine providence, Jeremiah about innocent suffering, Ezekiel about the power of repentance, and Second Isaiah about what it means to believe in a monotheistic conception of God. (For Job, keep reading.)

As in my previous book, *Thinking about the Torah: A Philosopher Reads the Bible* (JPS, 2016), I argue that to understand the full significance of prophetic literature, we have to move beyond the confines of the ancient Near East in which this literature is set and ask about the direction to which it is trying to point. Great ideas are not limited by time or place. Once they are put forward, they take on a life of their own. To look at that life and trace its progress is to read the prophets philosophically.

That is why, unlike most people who write about the prophets, I bring in the medieval and modern philosophers Maimonides, Kant, Cohen, Buber, Levinas, Heschel, and Soloveitchik, all of whom read the prophets and had important things to say as a result. Having moved beyond the ancient Near East, we can ask what the prophets have to teach us today.[2]

It is worth noting that all of the prophetic writings appear in the second of the Hebrew Bible's three sections (Torah, Prophets, and Writings) except Job, who is part of the third section. Unlike the books of the Prophets, which make reference to real people and historical events, the book of Job sets no historical context. In fact, it is not even clear that Job is an Israelite, because nothing is said about his lineage.[3] I have included a chapter on him not only because he intercedes with God on behalf of other people—as the prophets did—but because his plight raises a question that runs through much of prophetic literature, especially Jeremiah: Why would God allow an innocent person to suffer?

I do not claim that this book will resolve every question it raises and thereby end the need for further discussion. On the contrary, this book is meant to stimulate further discussion by highlighting issues that are too important to ignore. If we pray, what are we praying for and why? If we espouse a commitment to monotheism, what exactly does this entail? If we practice the rituals and remain loyal to tradition, do we have a right to expect that God will reward us in kind? No author will ever have the last word on these kinds of questions. But that is no excuse for ignoring them. If we do, I contend, religious practice will become rote and hypocritical—everything the prophets objected to.

Introduction

What Is a Prophet?

In a biblical context, a prophet (Hebrew *navi*) is a messenger or spokesperson for God.[1] The word "prophet" is derived from the Greek *prophetes*, which also means an "interpreter" or "spokesperson," typically someone who can read omens or who has received a divine communication (e.g., Teiresias in the plays of Sophocles). In simplest terms, then, a prophet is not someone who speaks in his or her own voice, but someone who has taken on the task of transmitting the voice of God. Much of the Bible consists of just such transmissions. As the biblical scholar James Kugel points out, the phrase "Thus says the LORD" occurs in the Bible more than three hundred times.[2]

Still there is more to prophecy than simply carrying a message from A to B. According to Abraham Joshua Heschel, a prophet is also a poet, preacher, patriot, statesman, social critic, and moralist.[3] Beyond that, prophets are people in their own right, which is to say individuals from a particular background, facing concrete questions such as when to go to war, how to respond to political and economic changes, what to say to priests, and whether judges and merchants are treating people fairly.

Understanding Prophecy

Today, many of us have trouble understanding prophecy because we live in a scientific culture far removed from the culture of our ancient ancestors. When we want to know about the weather, the outbreak of a dangerous epidemic, or the necessary preparations for war, we consult specialists with technical training. No such option was available to our ancestors. Nor was there a word in biblical Hebrew that corresponded to our word "nature" in the sense of a system of causes and effects that can be studied by the hypothetical/deductive method.

As a result, when the ancients needed advice, they looked to people who could relate God's intentions. If God wanted it to rain, they believed it would rain; if God wanted the Israelites to be victorious in battle, they would be victorious. Conversely, if God did not want the Israelites to be victorious, no amount of planning or exertion would help them.

Identifying a True Prophet

A key question for the ancients was how to identify a prophet. In Jewish tradition, Moses was (and is) considered the supreme prophet. It was Moses who served as the spokesperson, to whom God revealed the divine name, all the legislation of the Torah, the route of the Exodus, where and how to seek water in the desert, whom to attack, and, in a general way, whether the Israelites had remained faithful to the promises they made when they accepted the covenant.

Deuteronomy 18:15 tells us that God will raise up a prophet like Moses after the people enter the Promised Land ("The LORD your God will raise up for you a prophet from among your own people, like myself; him you shall heed"). But how will such a person be identified? Recall that, at the burning bush (Exod. 4), Moses worries that the people will not believe he has been sent by God. The answer, given in Deuteronomy, is that if a purported prophet speaks in the name of God and the prediction does not come to pass, then the person is a false prophet and should not be heeded. Deuteronomy 13 gives one qualification, however: If a purported prophet asks the people to follow strange gods, then even if the predictions come true, the person is a false prophet.

Unfortunately, these criteria still made it difficult for people to determine who was a true prophet and who was a pretender. Military powers rise and fall. Plagues can strike at any time. Floods and earthquakes take their toll as well. How long were the people to wait to decide if someone who predicted hardship, defeat, or disaster was telling the truth? Given sufficient time, almost any reasonable prediction would likely come true. As it is often said, even a broken clock is right twice every twenty-four hours.

The prophet Amos predicted the fall of the Northern Kingdom (Israel), which did indeed fall, but several decades later. At one point (8:8), he said the earth will shake. We know that his prophecy began some two years before an earthquake (1:1), but since he mentioned a variety of natural disasters, it is unclear whether "the earth will shake" referred to a specific event or was a general way of predicting misfortune. Nor is it clear how long this would go on or exactly how much damage it would cause.

In a passage from Isaiah (7:14–17) made famous by Christians, the prophet offered as a sign of his legitimacy the prediction that a young woman with child would give birth to a son named Immanuel and that by the time the child could distinguish between good and bad, the two foreign kings plotting against King Ahaz would have fallen and people would be eating curds and honey.[4] But, again, the details are unclear. Was Isaiah talking about a son born to Ahaz or to someone else? What exactly was the sign by which the people would know the child could distinguish between good and bad, and exactly when would it be fulfilled? We are not told. In another passage, Isaiah (31:5) predicted that Jerusalem would never fall. Although it did survive the siege of Sennacherib in 701 BCE, it fell to the Babylonians in 586 BCE.

To make the problem more difficult, Deuteronomy 18:9–14 warns that when the Israelites enter the Promised Land, they are not to pay attention to any augur, soothsayer, diviner, sorcerer, necromancer, one who casts spells, or one who consults with ghosts or spirits. These people, too, predict the future, and may get things right once in a while. Granted, they should be ignored if they ask people to follow strange gods, but what if they do not? What if they simply say they have the ability to see things other people cannot? How is one to tell which type of messenger is permitted and which forbidden?

Every age produces its share of dissident voices. Looking beyond the prophets, those voices include Socrates, Jesus, Yoḥanan ben Zakkai, Maimonides, Joan of Arc, Galileo, Spinoza, Thoreau, Gandhi, and Martin Luther King Jr., among others. It is easy for us to take these people seriously, because history has accorded them a privileged position. But it was not easy for their contemporaries to do so when they were alive. The same is true of the prophets. What criteria could one use to decide that Amos, Isaiah, and Jeremiah were legitimate, and their adversaries not?

The Varieties of Prophetic Experience

The problem of how to identify a true prophet was complicated by the fact that biblical prophets came in all shapes and sizes. According to a talmudic passage (*Megillah* 14a), there were forty-eight prophets and seven prophetesses in ancient Israel. In view of the importance of prophetic experience for Jewish self-understanding, medieval philosophers tried to devise a comprehensive theory encapsulating what prophecy consists of. Maimonides (1138–1204 CE) argued that the only way a person could get close enough to God to hear the divine voice was to develop her intellect to its fullest potential.[5] His reasoning was straightforward: A fool should never be trusted as a messenger of God. The only person we should trust is a person who understands what God is and the kinds of things God wants.

According to Maimonides, what distinguishes a normal person of learning, say a scientist or philosopher, from a prophet is that, in addition to having a perfected intellect, the prophet also has a lively or perfected imagination. That is why, unlike scientists or philosophers, prophets are able to use parables, metaphors, and vivid language to express themselves. One could give a reasoned argument on the virtues of peace and the horrors of war, but it would not have the same impact as the words of Isaiah 2:4: "And they shall beat their swords into plowshares / And their spears into pruning hooks." With this sort of example in mind, Maimonides goes on to say that the prophets' imaginations are so powerful that, instead of thinking only in abstract terms, they actually hear voices and see visions.

The obvious objection to this is that many of us hear voices at times or see visions in dreams, but that hardly makes us prophets. In response, Maimonides would say that the dreams or visions we have are disjointed and often incoherent. One night, we are running from terror; the next, we are sitting on top of the world. Rarely do our dreams have moral or religious significance. Rarer still is our ability to express them in poetic form using sophisticated literary techniques. For the prophets, it is otherwise. The voices or visions they experience contain messages of lasting importance, and the language in which their messages are expressed rivals that of the greatest poets of all time.

To Maimonides, the lively imagination that served as a prerequisite for prophecy was a natural gift; if a person did not have one, there was nothing she could do to get it. When it comes to perfecting the intellect, however, Maimonides thought that only a person who lived a moral life and exercised a high degree of self-control could devote the time and energy needed to master whole bodies of knowledge. Again his reasoning was straightforward: Why would God reveal something to a thug or a libertine?

It is clear, however, that Maimonides' theory runs into problems. If prophecy involves perfection of the intellect, we would expect it to be widespread among the educated elite; but experience indicates that this is not so. Nor is it true that every person who became a prophet is a moral exemplar. Although no evidence suggests that Hagar, Sarah's maidservant, had low moral standards, neither is there evidence that she was an intellectual giant—and yet, God sends an angel to address her at Genesis 21:17–18. From what we can tell, Balaam, a sorcerer hired to curse the Jewish people, did have low moral standards, but God addresses him several times at Numbers 22–24. By contrast, Joseph was a person of high moral standards who carried out the will of God, yet he never hears God's voice. As Rabbi Barry Schwartz points out, there are also biblical figures who, though not prophets in their own right, possess prophet-like qualities: the seer (*roeh*), visionary (*khozeh*), and man of God (*ish-Elohim*).[6] Still others, like Joseph, are people of high moral standards and therefore heroes in the prophetic mold, for example, Caleb, Hannah, and Ruth.

Even if we stick to people designated as prophets, it is difficult to construct a single theory accounting for all of them. Some prophets (e.g., Nathan) served by royal appointment, while others took money for their services.[7] By the time of Samuel, there were prophetic guilds or schools where people may have received something in the way of formal training.[8] King Ahab had four hundred prophets advise him when to go to war — almost as large a group as the U.S. House of Representatives. Not surprisingly, they spoke in one voice and told him exactly what he wanted to hear (1 Kings 22). A lone dissenter, the prophet Micaiah, mocks the unanimity of the others and correctly predicts disaster for Ahab.

Though some prophets probably received training, Amos, the first of the prophets who wrote down their messages and personal histories in literary form, did not. During his confrontation with the High Priest he declares: "I am not a prophet, and I am not a prophet's disciple [son of a prophet]" (7:14). This may be taken to mean that he was not a member of a guild and did not have any official status. As he relays in the next sentence, he is a cattle breeder and a tender of sycamore figs. In all likelihood, he was not poor; his facility with language suggests that he must have been educated. Perhaps he ran something like the ancient equivalent of a farm or ranch. But neither was he a professional when it came to religious matters.

Looking at the rest of the Bible, we also learn of prophetic trances or frenzies whose states were so powerful that the people who witnessed them could easily be drawn in. To take a noteworthy example, Saul becomes possessed by such a frenzy and, in one instance, is so taken with it that he lies naked all day and all night (1 Sam. 10:10, 19:18–24). 1 Samuel 10:5 tells us that such states were brought on by musical instruments, which could indicate that rhythmic dancing was also part of the experience.[9] Some scholars speculate that the priestess at Delphi, who served as a prophetess for the ancient Greeks, went into a trance by breathing intoxicating vapors.[10] Even in the case of Abraham (Gen. 15:12), the Torah says that a deep sleep and "a great dark dread descended upon him" before God spoke.

Although we may question Maimonides' attempt to subsume all prophetic experiences under one theory, he is right to point out that nothing like a trance or state of intoxication applies to Moses. At Numbers 12:6–8, God explains why Moses' prophecy is unique: "When a prophet of the LORD arises among you, I make myself known to him in a vision, I speak with him in a dream. Not so with My servant Moses; he is trusted throughout My household. With him I speak mouth to mouth, plainly not in riddles." This means that Moses achieved a degree of clarity and specificity that the other prophets lacked. There is no mention here of ecstasy or possession. As far as we can tell, Moses is wide awake and in full possession of his faculties every time God speaks to him. In some passages, he is even willing to question God.

The record is equally mixed when it comes to miracles. The Bible tells us that both Elijah and Elisha performed miracles, including raising people from the dead (1 Kings 17–24; 2 Kings 4: 18–37). But there is nothing comparable in the literary prophets that are discussed in this book. As the biblical scholar Richard Elliott Friedman points out, Elijah is the last person in the Bible to produce a large-scale public miracle of the sort produced by Moses.[11] That is not to say that there are no miracles after Elijah, but that they are either private (e.g., Jonah's captivity in the belly of the fish) or comparatively small (e.g., Isaiah's causing a sundial to move ten steps backward).

We saw that if a prophet means someone addressed by God, then Hagar and Balaam qualify as prophets, though neither was an Israelite. Although Maimonides recognizes the possibility of gentile prophets, not every Jewish thinker would agree.[12] His predecessor Judah Halevi (1075–1141) restricted prophecy to Jews, even to Jews residing in the Land of Israel.[13]

It is noteworthy that in the midst of a male-dominated culture, the Bible mentions four female prophets: Miriam (Exod. 15:20), Deborah (Judg. 4:4), Huldah (2 Kings 22:14–20 and 2 Chron. 34:22–28), and Noadiah (Neh. 6:14). Although none of the literary prophets whose works are preserved were women, the prophetic status of Miriam and the others does not seem to have caused a problem among their contemporaries. No one said that Deborah could not be a prophet because she was a woman.

From a sociological perspective, the word of God came to Moses when he was an adult criminal living in exile, to Jeremiah when he was probably a teenager. Hagar was a servant. We saw that Amos was a breeder of cattle; on the other hand, Ezekiel was a priest, and Isaiah (or the first prophet to go under that name) may have been a priest as well.[14] Little is known about Hosea. Although most kings inherited their positions as a result of birth, the political theorist Michael Walzer points out that none of the literary prophets did; instead of being born into their roles, they were called by God.[15] Not only were they called, to continue with Walzer's insight, they do not get to name their successors.[16]

In view of the diversity of prophets, it is difficult to decide who is a true prophet on external factors alone. Some of the people mentioned above, for example, Ahab's four-hundred-member prophetic consortium, had to have been fakes; they reinforced the king's own beliefs and their prediction turned out to be false. The same may have been true of those who demanded money for their services, a group for whom Micah (3:5-11) had nothing but contempt. Ultimately, it all depends on whom God picks to carry the message. In many cases, that person may not be the one we would expect God to choose, but that likely says more about us than it does about God.

Predicting the Future or Exhorting Behavior?

As we saw, one simple answer to the question of how to identify a true prophet is to assess the accuracy of the purported prophet's predictions. As we use the word today, a prophet is usually someone who can tell us what the future has in store before anyone else. Many biblical prophets were consulted in order to get specific information about politics, weather conditions, or the outcome of battles. Some were even thought to be able to locate lost articles.

Yet when it comes to the great prophets who make up the subject matter of this book, the question of prediction is complicated. First, some background. Although biblical Hebrew had no word corresponding to *"nature"* as we understand it, the ancient Greeks did—*physis*. In fact, science as we know it was largely a Greek discovery. Once someone understands how nature operates and assumes that it is everywhere and always the same, it becomes possible to make predictions. Given the molecular structure of water, one can predict when it will freeze. Given the mass of the moon, one can predict how strong its gravitational pull will be. Given the mass and chemical make-up of the sun, one can predict that it in a billion years or so, it will become so hot that life on earth will cease.

It is often said that the origin of our concept of natural necessity derives from the Greek concept of Fate (*Moira*). According to mythology, the Fates determined the length and outcome of a person's life so that no one—not even the gods—could interfere. Thus Oedipus is fated to kill his father and marry his mother. In the *Iliad* (16:419–61), when it is time for the Trojan warrior Sarpedon to die, Zeus asks whether he should intervene but is told that if he does, chaos will result. Even though Zeus is the most powerful god on Mount Olympus, he can only sit back and watch. Our concept of nature took shape from this idea of an underlying necessity that governs the world order. Rather than look to the gods as an explanation for why it rained, early Greek thinkers came up with a different explanation: Changes in weather are the result of condensation and rarefaction.

The prophets did not see things this way. Their predictions of impending doom were not like a scientist's prediction of what will happen to the sun in a billion years. For the prophets, the order of the world is moral, not mechanical.[17] The mountains will shake and the rivers run dry *unless* the people change their ways and return to God. Thus Jonah warns the people of Nineveh that their city is about to be destroyed; but the people repent, God undergoes a change of mind, and the city is saved. While in some places, for example, Isaiah 6:10 and Ezekiel 2:7, God, having suffered countless acts of rebellion, becomes so angry that the prophet is instructed to speak even though the people will not listen, these passages can be viewed as limiting cases rather than direct counterexamples. In other words, God may be saying that the people have made the wrong choice so many times in the past that it is all but hopeless to expect them to make the right choice in the present. In short, the people's recalcitrance is the problem, not an unbreakable necessity imposed from above.

We can therefore agree with Heschel when he says that the prominent theme of the prophets is exhortation, not simple prediction.[18] According to Kugel, the change in emphasis from exhortation to prediction began in the Second Temple period, in large part because predictions were allowed to range over a much longer period.[19] But as the length of the period expanded, it became increasingly difficult to know how a prediction could be disconfirmed, since all one had to say is, "Give it more time." The prophets aimed to paint a bleak picture of the future so the people would take note of what they were doing in the present. But, again, how long were they supposed to wait to verify their prognostications? Such considerations led the biblical scholar Yehezkel Kaufmann to conclude that the agreement between prophecy and historical reality "does not extend to details."[20]

This brings us back to our central question: How do we know when someone is actually speaking for God? A partial answer may be found at Jeremiah 28:1–17, when an argument breaks out between two prophets, Jeremiah and Hananiah. The former predicts doom, the latter good fortune. Both spoke in the Temple and began their prophecies with the words, "Thus says the LORD." Which one should the people follow? Jeremiah responds that, given the many predictions of war, disaster, and pestilence that preceded him, it is more likely that he, rather than his opponent, is telling the truth.[21] He goes on to say that we should be skeptical of prophets who predict good fortune, and believe them only if what they say actually comes to pass. As it happens, Jeremiah was right: Jerusalem fell to the Babylonians eight years later.[22] But how could the people have known this at the time?

In an earlier passage (23:9–40), Jeremiah gives the gist of an answer. Pay no heed to a prophet whose words do not exhort the people to turn from evil and pursue goodness. The problem with predictions of good fortune is they run the risk of moral complacency. It is all too easy to think: things are going to turn out well, so there is no need to alter my behavior. While true prophets also hold out messages of consolation, they do so in the belief that injustice will be eradicated and eventually the people will return to God. Despite passage after passage predicting doom, Jeremiah himself foresees a time when God will make a new covenant with the people: "I will put my law within them, and I will write it on their hearts; and I will be their God" (31:31–34).

Putting all this together, we arrive at the conclusion that it is not so much the prophets' ability to predict the future that establishes their credentials as the moral fiber of their message. They refuse to believe that God is satisfied with the behavior they see around them—whether in Israel or the other nations of the earth. The idea of a God willing to look the other way as the poor are trampled on, judges bought off, and merchants cheat their customers is abhorrent. The same is true of a God who sees injustice but can be appeased by sacrificing animals or burning incense.

A good example of this point can be found in the memorable words of Zechariah (4:6): "Not by might, nor by power, but by My spirit— said the LORD of Hosts." Whatever history tells us about the use of raw power to decide international disputes, the prophet is telling us: This is not the right way to do it. Might does not make right, and if God stands for anything, it is for what is right.

Often the prophets' words are scathing. Hosea accused the people of whoring (4:10–12). Isaiah accused the people, including priests and (false) prophets, of drunkenness (28:1–8). Jeremiah was told that God is so angry with the people, he should not intercede on their behalf (7:16). To be sure, no one likes to be dressed down in public, especially by a person claiming to speak for God. Nonetheless, even these words of the prophets represent attempts to appeal to our conscience, what Jeremiah called "the law inscribed on our hearts" (31:33). The prophets are relying on our sense that no matter how hard their words are to hear, we know they are right: the poor are not treated properly, the courts are not completely impartial, dishonest practices in the marketplace are all too common. This cannot be what God wants, and if the will of God eventually prevails, then someday justice will be done.

In one sense this is a prediction, but unlike a scientific prediction, which assumes an orderly connection between the present and future, this one assumes that if the people heed the message, the future will be radically different from the present: behavior as it is now will be transformed into behavior as it ought to be. It follows that rather than looking to external factors such as age, social status, or professional training, rather than keeping close tabs on whether a prediction has come true, the only hope for identifying a true prophet is to consider the moral truth of the message. If we follow Maimonides, we also would have to look for a lively imagination and a memorable facility with words. But the communication of moral truth is the primary factor.

Needless to say, assessing moral truth is not always easy to do. Even to begin, one must ask what morality requires. But difficult as the process is, there is no real alternative. Following Jeremiah, a person who assures us that we are doing the right thing and there is nothing to worry about in the days ahead, a person who lures us into a feeling of complacency, cannot be a prophet.

Are There Any Modern-Day Prophets?

In putting a complicated subject like prophecy under the microscope, it often happens that we answer one question only to raise another. If prophets are to be identified primarily by the moral truth of their message, why do we generally not refer to people as prophets today? Why aren't people like Thoreau, Gandhi, King, or Heschel—who marched with King and took on the task of shocking modern Jews out of their supposed state of complacency—considered prophets?

The traditional Jewish position, as articulated by the Rabbis, is that the age of prophecy came to an end with Malachi (500–450 BCE), roughly three hundred years after it began.[23] This position seems to be confirmed by the prophet Zachariah (13:2–4), who predicts that in anger, God will rid the land of prophets. Along these lines, 1 Maccabees (9:27) relates that at the time of the Second Temple: "There was great distress in Israel, such as had not been seen since the time that prophets ceased to appear among them." One Rabbinic source (*Bava Batra* 12b) maintains that since the destruction of the Second Temple, prophecy was taken from the prophets and given over to children and fools.

Why would a movement that produced some of the most creative and far-reaching literature the world has ever known suddenly die out? Was God displeased with Israel? The prophets often picture God as exasperated with the people and ready to take drastic measures against them. Having revealed God's will at Sinai, and sent the likes of Moses, Joshua, Deborah, Samuel, David, Solomon, Amos, Isaiah, and Jeremiah to offer guidance, God cannot understand why the people still do not heed the right message. As the author of 2 Chronicles (36:15–16) put it: "The LORD God of their fathers had sent word to them through His messengers daily without fail, for He had pity on His people and His dwelling-place. But they mocked the messengers of God and disdained His prophets until the wrath of the LORD against His people grew beyond remedy."[24]

Did God really become dissatisfied with the Jewish people? Heschel opposed this view, arguing that medieval figures, including Maimonides, received mystical or esoteric knowledge that they understood as given to them by God.[25] In other words, Heschel thought the idea that there was a cutoff when God suddenly decided not to address people anymore makes no sense. He is right to the degree that throughout Jewish history, the word "prophet" has been used to cover a variety of people and religious experiences. The broader issue here is whether it makes sense to draw a line between the great prophets of old, such as Amos, Isaiah, and Jeremiah, and people of learning and inspiration who came after them.

It is noteworthy that in Maimonides' masterpiece, the *Guide of the Perplexed*, he twice denies that he is the beneficiary of prophetic insight, while in the *Mishneh Torah*, his great compendium of Jewish law, he says that anyone who supports an interpretation of Jewish law by saying that God spoke to him should be put to death.[26] Though he allows that there may be prophets at a future date, he argues that their role is restricted to issues like when to go to war or where to build a well.

Beyond these admissions, there is the vast difference between the climate in which the prophets composed their writings and that in which

Maimonides composed his. While it is unclear how much of the Torah and the other biblical books the prophets had access to, the prophets were able to proclaim "Thus says the LORD" because they lived in a period in which the record of what God said was still fresh and open to new additions.[27] Looking at the Torah, we find that in the book of Genesis, God or one of the angels speaks to people all the time. By the time we get to the book of Exodus, dialogues between heaven and earth take up much of the narrative. We saw that in Numbers (12:6–8) God makes a distinction between Moses and the other prophets, saying that the latter encounter God in dreams or visions rather than face to face. The last time that the divine cloud or glory (*kavod*) of God appears in the Bible is at the dedication of Solomon's Temple (1 Kings 8:11). We also saw that according to Friedman, there is a cessation of public miracles after Elijah and Elisha.[28] All of this is of a piece with his claim that as we move through the Bible, God becomes ever more distant. By the time we get to the book of Esther, God does not appear at all.

In a famous passage from the Talmud (*Bava Metzi'a* 59b), God enters into a legal dispute between two famous rabbis but is told that, on the basis of Deuteronomy 30:11, which says that the Torah is not in heaven, the divine voice has no standing in court. If God has no standing in court, then neither does a prophet who speaks in the name of God—hence Maimonides' view that anyone who violates this rule should be put to death. As previously mentioned, Maimonides saw the role of future prophets as limited to issues such as when to go to war or where to build a well. Clearly, modern military science and geology have made such assistance unnecessary.

One way to approach the question of why prophecy ceased is to recognize that as the Jewish religion developed, more and more texts joined the canon of what counted as sacred literature. Tradition holds that 613 individual commandments were given in the Torah. Commentary on how those commandments were to be understood and applied began soon thereafter. Before long, there was commentary on the commentary, and commentary on the commentary on the commentary. Maimonides was as much a part of this tradition as anyone else. So in his day was

Heschel. As layer after layer of commentary built up, it was inevitable that the prophet would give way to the exegete. And although the exegete may have been inspired, his claim was not that he had been given the word of God but that he could decipher the will of God on the basis of a close reading of what had already been recorded.[29]

As a result, most people today would be skeptical of someone who claimed to hear God's voice directly. If we hear God, we tend to believe it is through the medium of the written word rather than the spoken word. It is no accident, then, that the phrase "Thus says the LORD" is no longer in use even by moderns with profound spiritual convictions. Rather than messengers in the biblical sense of the term, we have preachers, witnesses, spokespeople, or moral teachers.

Clearly there is a measure of overlap. It does not take much imagination to picture one of the prophets sitting at a racially segregated lunch counter in Alabama or engaging in a nonviolent protest against involvement in a foreign war. Still, overlap is not the same as identity. In our day and age, important dissident voices are more likely to quote the Bible than to think of themselves as standing on equal footing with its most famous authors.

In the end, we might do well to stick to the division Hillel made between prophets and the children of prophets. Let us therefore say that by holding people to high moral standards and calling attention to injustice, the "children of prophets," people like Thoreau, Gandhi, and Heschel who exhibited a similar cast of mind, played a role in their societies similar to the role the prophets played in ancient times.

Prophecy and Religious Renewal

Even if we accept the view that prophecy came to an end in the ancient world, there may still be a need to infuse the religion of today with a greater sense of spontaneity. The biblical canon was closed a long time ago. The prayers have become standardized. For traditional Jews, they are said three times a day, seven days a week. While the familiarity of the prayers may provide a degree of comfort or a sense of belonging, their constant repetition can impair the practice of saying them with any degree of feeling, or with what the Rabbis called *kavanah* (intention).

Considerations like these motivated the twentieth-century thinker Martin Buber's study of prophecy, first published in English in 1949. As he put it: "Centralization and codification, undertaken in the interests of religion, are a danger to the core of religion, unless there is the strongest life of faith, embodied in the whole of existence of the community, and not relaxing in its renewing activity."[30]

What is that faith? For Buber it meant being open to the experience of wonder, which is to say "an event which cannot be grasped except as an act of God."[31] This is not the distant God loved by philosophers, but an active God who enters into human history and seeks to facilitate a dialogue with human beings. The writings of the prophets are a record of that dialogue. Although they articulated eternal truths, Buber was at pains to show that rather than teach theological lessons as we might understand them, the prophets responded to God by putting specific choices before the people.[32] Still today, he believed, we, the Jewish nation, can continue doing what we have been doing, or we can undergo a change of heart and strike out in a new direction—one that puts aside the allures of politics and economics and allows us to see our task as becoming a holy nation dedicated to serving God.

A choice is a call to action. Rather than repeat established formulas or theological dogmas, Buber envisioned a renewal of the spirit that motivated the prophets to trust God and called the people to account for themselves. In one place, he went so far as to say that God does not attach decisive importance to the things normally grouped under the term "religion."[33] As he saw it, pagan gods were dependent on things like houses, altars, and sacrificial worship because these things were tangible symbols of their importance. While the God of Israel might have asked our ancestors for similar things, from Buber's perspective, God does not really need them. Instead of "religion," what God wants is "the makers of decision vindicating their right to those thirsting for justice, the strong having pity on the weak."[34] In short, by reading the prophets we learn that the need to rethink our values and rededicate ourselves to the things in life that really matter is as pressing for us as it was for people in ancient times.

The Prophetic Legacy

The prophets speak to us from a distant age. Beyond the question of textuality, there is the ever-present question of science. People who predict plagues, droughts, or military uprisings now have to answer to specialists in command of large bodies of empirical evidence. Again, within this framework, "Thus says the LORD" will not get one very far.

Still, we do the prophets an injustice if we fail to recognize the lasting validity of their messages. When they insist on justice, express compassion for the poor, or tell us that we have it within our power to put our past mistakes behind us and set out on a new course, I would argue that they *do* speak for God. Their messages were as authentic then as they are now. That is why it is important that we study them closely and ask ourselves what these messages are trying to say. In my opinion, we can do this by examining the principles that lie behind the messages they received, not by claiming to be recipients of new ones.

THINKING ABOUT THE PROPHETS

CHAPTER 1

Amos

Moral Idealism

I loathe, I spurn your festivals,
I am not appeased by your solemn assemblies
If you offer Me burnt offerings — or your meal offerings —
I will not accept them;
I will pay no heed
To your gifts of fatlings.
Spare Me the sound of your hymns,
And let Me not hear the music of your lutes.
But let justice well up like water,
Righteousness like an unfailing stream.

—AMOS 5:21–24

Amos, the first of the literary prophets, sets the tone for much that follows. He proclaims that God will not tolerate injustice or religious hypocrisy, that God will exact a terrible punishment if the people do not change their ways, and yet that eventually God will relent, restore the Davidic dynasty, and rebuild Israel.[1]

We can learn much about Amos's thought by looking at the times in which he lived. His prophecy took place in the eighth century BCE, when the Israelite people were divided between a Northern and a Southern Kingdom. Although Amos came from Tekoa, a small town in the South, his message was addressed to the people of the North. Exactly why is unclear. History records that in Amos's day, the Northern Kingdom had expanded its territory, which implies that the economy must have been thriving. In chapter 6, Amos refers to richly adorned summer and winter houses, lavish furnishings, sumptuous meals, ample quantities of wine, and the choicest of oils. Furthermore, we know from chapters 4 and 7 that there was a shrine at Bethel presided over by a priest, that sacrifices were offered there, and that festivals were observed.

In other words, these were times of happiness and prosperity. And therein lies a lesson for us. It may be easy for us to understand how God can be angry with people when times are rough. Who has not looked to heaven and asked "What have I done wrong?" when faced with misfortune? In good times, though, there is an equally powerful tendency to think that God must be pleased. If, then, the Northern Kingdom was prospering, and the sacrifices and the festivals were being observed, the priest and the rest of the nation must have thought that they were doing something right.

Against this presumption, the crux of Amos's message is that the pride that comes with good fortune is illusory unless it is supported by moral conduct. It is illusory because God is not impressed by finely adorned houses if the poor are not cared for and because the prosperity that people enjoy today may vanish tomorrow. In short, Amos is warning us that human happiness is not an infallible guide to divine judgment. God may be close to those who suffer and indignant with those who prosper (as we shall see throughout this book). Rather than happiness, the true guide to divine judgment is morality. Hence the words quoted in the opening of the chapter: "Let justice well up like water / Righteousness like an unfailing stream."[2]

The Indictment

Amos begins his prophecy with stinging criticisms of the neighbors of the Northern and Southern Kingdoms. In their quest for political power, they have broken treaties, sent whole populations into exile, shown no mercy to their victims, and committed a host of other atrocities. For example, Amos (1:6) predicts that God will smite the Philistines with fire. Buber would later write that the interesting thing about God's criticism of the other nations is not that God is displeased with their offenses against the Divine, but at their offenses against each other.[3] In any event, Amos's audience was likely delighted to hear about the sins of their neighbors and how God would punish them.

At the very least, the indictment of other nations shows that God is concerned with more than just the fortunes of Israel but insists on moral standards that are valid for everyone. Later, Amos emphasizes the universality of God's reach in even stronger terms:

> To Me, O Israelites, you are
> Just like the Ethiopians — declares the LORD.
> True, I brought Israel up
> From the Land of Egypt.
> But also the Philistines from Caphor
> And the Arameans from Kir. (9:7)

In short, Israel is not the only nation to have experienced an exodus. God also liberated the Philistines and Arameans. And yet, for all that, God has a special relationship with Israel (3:2): "You alone have I singled out / Of all the families of the earth."

This not does mean that Israel will get off lightly. After the indictment of other nations in the opening chapter, Amos makes clear that God is just as angry with Israel—perhaps more so. In fact, the passage that begins "You alone have I singled out" finishes with: "That is why I will call you to account / For all your iniquities." If Israel has been chosen among all the nations of the earth, God expects more from it, not less.

What exactly is the problem? Amos does not mince words. The people defraud the poor and rob the needy. They take bribes and use false weights and measures in the marketplace. They impose high taxes on the poor. Although they take off from work on the Sabbath and festivals, instead of focusing on the religious significance of these days, all they can think about is getting back to the marketplace and continuing to cheat people. The references to excessive eating and drinking suggest that decadence was common. Worse, the people think they can get away with anything as long as they offer sacrifices to God. So biting is Amos's criticism, he is not above using sarcasm to make his point:

> Come to Bethel [location of a holy shrine] and transgress;
> To Gilgal [another shrine], and transgress even more:
> Present your sacrifices the next morning
> And your tithes on the third day;
> And burn a thank offering of leavened bread,
> And proclaim freewill offerings loudly.
> For you love that sort of thing, O Israelites. (4:4–5)

Religious practice, then, has become a sham, an outward display of piety that does nothing to motivate better behavior, and therefore is hateful to God. People who have sinned cannot put themselves in God's good graces merely by slaughtering an animal, even if the slaughtering is done according to accepted rules of sacrifice.

How was the message received? When Amos confronts Amaziah, the priest at Bethel, he hears that his message is subversive and that he must leave the Northern Kingdom immediately (7:10–11). The reason given for the banishment is Amos's prediction: God is about to judge the Northern Kingdom and see through its hypocrisy, at which point the king will die by the sword, and the people will be conquered by a foreign power. We should keep in mind that Amaziah served the king, and his authority was being challenged by an outsider with no recognizable credentials. And yet for all this, it is Amos, the cattle breeder, who earns an important place in history; Amaziah, the priest, is all but forgotten.

There is no evidence that Amos wanted to eliminate the sacrificial cult altogether, or do away with other forms of religious observance. However distasteful animal sacrifice may be to us today, we should not forget that it had deep spiritual significance to our ancestors. It was their chief way of establishing closeness to God—either by seeking atonement or expressing thanksgiving. As Maimonides pointed out, a religion without sacrifice would have seemed as empty to them as a religion without prayer does to us.[4]

What Amos objects to is not sacrifice as such but the belief that it can atone for cruelty and injustice all by itself—that all one has to do to stay in God's good graces is show up for the festivals, bring an animal to be slaughtered, and sing the usual hymns. His point is that God wants more than this. If you want to please a God who insists on justice, then you have to insist on it as well. If you turn a blind eye to the treatment of the poor, then all the sacrifices in the world will not accomplish anything.

From a philosophic perspective, Amos is saying that sacrifice is not an end in itself. One cannot say, "I have offered my sacrifice and now I can return to business as usual." Rather, sacrifice is valuable to the degree that it leads to or is combined with a sincere desire to serve God—or, as the Bible says in several places, to walk in the ways of God.[5] To be sure, God goes to great lengths to describe the proper way to conduct worship and is not pleased when the rules are broken.[6] But above and beyond the rules of worship, God does not like hypocritical religion, which is to say religion that is not combined with moral behavior. The problem for the people, of course, is that sacrificing an animal is a relatively simple act, whereas improving one's behavior takes considerable effort.

To bring this point up to date, the same perspective applies to prayer. Just as God is not satisfied with sacrifice that is not combined with moral behavior, so God is not satisfied with moving one's lips as the sole way of atoning for sin. This is true even if the words one utters are full of praise for God and beg God for mercy. Whether we are talking about sacrifice, prayer, or some other form of religious observance, the only way to reinstate oneself with God is to make a concerted effort to become a better person. Prayer can help if one enters into it in a spirit of contrition, but in no sense can it be a shortcut or a substitute for turning one's behavior around.

The Punishment

A basic rule of jurisprudence is that the severity of the punishment should match the severity of the crime. As Amos sees it, the crime is no small matter. Rather than accuse the people of procedural violations in their religious practice, he charges them with perverting the cause of justice:

> They have sold for silver
> Those whose cause is just,
> And the needy for [the price of] a pair of sandals.
> [Ah,] you who trample the heads of the poor
> Into the dust of the ground,
> And make the humble walk a twisted course! (2:6–7)

As normally understood, justice has two dimensions. The first involves honesty in dealings with other people; thus, one is not to engage in bribery, fraudulent business practices, and the like. The second involves an equitable distribution of society's resources; thus, one must steer clear of excessive taxation, selling people into slavery for failing to pay trivial sums of money, and facilitating conditions that contribute to vast differences between rich and poor. Having offended God on both counts, the people deserve considerably more than the proverbial slap on the wrist.

It should be understood that the punishment Amos is talking about is not like that handed out to a criminal after the jury returns a guilty verdict. God is not seeking revenge, but reform. Once again, the punishment should be understood along the lines of an exhortation: *This* is what will happen to you unless you alter your conduct. As the prophet Ezekiel (18:23) put it years later, God does not desire the death of sinners, only that they change their ways.

So understood, Amos's prediction of what will happen is contingent on the people's not heeding God's warning:

> I will make the sun set at noon,
> I will darken the earth on a sunny day.
> I will turn your festivals into mourning
> And your songs into dirges;
> I will put sackcloth on all loins

And tonsures on every head.
I will make it [the earth] mourn as for an only child,
All of it as on a bitter day. (8:9–10)

In addition to its severity, Amos's vision of divine retribution is note-worthy for the cosmic nature of its scope. In an environment where people worshiped multiple gods, each god or goddess had a particular area over which he or she held sway, for instance, a river, a mountain, or a forest. In Greek mythology, for example, Hades ruled the under-world, Poseidon the sea, and Zeus the sky. To be sure, the acceptance of monotheism did not occur all at once, but proceeded in stages (see chapter 7). But when it finally took hold, what emerged is the idea that one God is responsible for all of creation, and therefore rules over every nation and geographic region. In Amos's words:

If they burrow down to Sheol [the netherworld]
From there My hand shall take them;
And if they ascend to heaven,
From there I will bring them down.
If they hide on the top of Carmel,
There I will search them out and seize them;
And if they conceal themselves from My sight
At the bottom of the sea,
There I will command
The serpent to bite them. (9:2–4)

As Jonah learned, it is impossible to flee from such a God. And, we might add, it is equally impossible to deceive God. In another passage (3:6), Amos goes so far as to say that the people's entire fortunes are in the hands of God: "Does disaster befall a city, / unless God has done it?" If this is true, it makes no difference whether the city is destroyed by an earthquake or a foreign power; in either case, God is responsible.

For modern readers, the tendency to see the hand of God behind every misfortune creates a serious problem (see the fuller discussion in chapter 3). For the present, it is enough to realize that when we move from polytheism to monotheism, we give up the possibility that there is any force in the universe that can prevent God's will from being realized. One can ask God for leniency, as Moses does after the people turn to the Golden Calf and Amos does twice at 7:1–4 ("How will Jacob survive? He is so small"). But once God has reached a decision, as happens at 7:7–9 ("I will pardon them no more"), nothing can stand in the way.

As is the rule in prophetic literature, the severity of the punishment is tempered by the vision of a better future:

> But, I will not wholly wipe out
> The House of Jacob — declares the LORD. . . .
> I will restore My people Israel.
> They shall rebuild ruined cities and inhabit them;
> They shall plant vineyards and drink their wine;
> They shall till gardens and eat their fruits.
> And I will plant them upon their soil,
> Nevermore to be uprooted
> From the soil I have given them. (9:8–15)[7]

These lines would make no sense unless they implied that there were enough righteous people in Israel — a holy remnant — for God to maintain the special relationship with the nation. Elsewhere (5:3), Amos suggests that the number of the righteous amounts to 10 percent of the population. In time, the belief that God would uphold the covenant if even a small percentage of Israel upheld its part would sustain the Jewish people through multiple periods of crisis.

Be Realistic!

One does not have to dig very deeply to see that Amos's indictment raises an important question. According to his account, the Northern Kingdom had reached a state of almost total depravity. The prophet Hosea, a contemporary of Amos, made a similar appraisal:

There is no honesty and no goodness
And no obedience to God in the land.
[False] swearing, dishonesty, and murder,
And theft and adultery are rife;
Crime follows upon crime! (Hosea 4:1–2)

Was this true? Was the Northern Kingdom any worse than its neighbors, than other Jewish communities before and afterward, or, for that matter, any society for which we have historical records? Isaiah (1:10) compares the Southern Kingdom to Sodom and Gomorrah. Jeremiah (23:11) says that both the priests and prophets of Jerusalem are godless and that their wickedness extends even to the Temple. Ezekiel (16:47–52) maintains that, next to Jerusalem, Sodom does not seem all that bad.

Here, one is inclined to ask: Where is the society that has completely eliminated bribery, dishonesty, and murder? Where are the poor and powerless given the respect they deserve? In what community do worshipers or even priests serve God with complete sincerity? As Yehezkel Kaufmann notes, these shortcomings are found everywhere and in every age.[8] Furthermore, where is the evidence that the Northern and Southern Kingdoms were any worse than the other nations that eventually conquered them?

To my mind, Heschel is right to say that if the situation were as bad as the prophets would have us believe, other sources, for example, the books of Kings, would have pointed it out.[9] Rather than Israel having hit a low point in the history of the ancient Near East, it is more likely that when it comes to the prophets, we are dealing with people of pronounced moral sensitivity, people who believe that if Israel is to be a light unto the other nations, it must be judged by a higher standard. By their own admission, the prophets are tasked with carrying out the words of God. It is not surprising, then, that injustices that some of us would brush off on the grounds that no one is perfect set them ablaze.

At bottom, the prophets claim that *any* injustice is intolerable, and, no doubt they are right. When interpreting their messages, however, we cannot lose sight of what is humanly possible and what is not. Who has ever come to God with completely pure hands or a completely pure heart? If the answer is no one, why should we judge society by insurmountable standards? Why should we not set standards which, though not perfect, are at least attainable?

The answer, as Heschel goes on to say, is that the prophets are not comfortable with a middle-of-the-road approach.[10] This much is clear from the force of their rhetoric and the dire nature of their warnings. The question raised by the severity of Amos's words has to do with how we establish moral standards. One view is that it is unrealistic to establish such standards without taking existing behavior into consideration.

Behind this view is the claim that if moral standards expect too much of people, if they ask for unachievable behavior, then people are likely to disregard them. Suppose people in your community, gathered in a public space, heard a modern-day prophet exhort them to give away most of their possessions, refrain from eating elaborate meals, and contribute half of their income to charity. Although one or two people in the crowd might follow such advice, in all likelihood, wouldn't most of them ignore it? In view of this, would it not be more prudent to offer advice in keeping with what has some chance of success?

In the Torah, there is a marked difference in the environments in which Moses and his brother, Aaron, serve God. Moses speaks to God alone on a mountaintop, without special clothing, gold, jewels, or an elaborately constructed place of worship. As the High Priest, Aaron makes use of all these things. Although one could argue that Moses was closer to God and therefore represents the highest form of worship, the number of people capable of serving God without such accoutrements is extremely limited. Most of us need the beauty and solemnity provided by special clothes and luxuriously constructed surroundings. As Maimonides speculates, the Israelites may not have been ready for an austere form of religion and needed something closer to the kind of religion they observed in Egypt.[11] So rather than asking people to ascend a mountain and go without food or water, God commanded the construction of a Tabernacle and joyous festivals.

Even when it comes to the specifics of a legal code—whether secular or religious—there is a question of whether the law should set an ideal standard or reflect the attitudes and practices already in place. *Merriam-Webster's Collegiate Dictionary* seems to recognize both. It defines law as "a binding custom or practice of a community" but then offers as an alternative definition: "a rule of conduct or action *prescribed* [my italics] or formally recognized as binding."

In many ways, the ancient Rabbis were realists. When they could not resolve a dispute among themselves, they sometimes decided the matter by looking at existing behavior.[12] Hillel does this in the aforementioned passage where he says that we are the children of prophets. In other contexts, the Rabbis invoked a principle according to which one should not make a decree unless the majority of the public are able to observe it.[13] They reasoned that if the law were too far ahead of the people, it would turn large numbers of them into sinners. On the other hand, there is no denying that some commandments, for example, love of God, fear of God, and love of one's neighbor, set standards that only the most pious can approach.

Philosophers have debated this question as well. On the side of those who ask for realistic standards are Aristotle (484–322 BCE) and, in a later age, Hegel (1770–1831). Aristotle insisted that we cannot understand what justice is without looking at the constitutions of existing states and asking how they conduct their business. Needless to say, the culture in which he lived was infused with aristocratic values. At one place in his ethical writings, he asks whether it is possible, or at least not easy, to live a completely successful life without external goods such as friends, wealth, political power, high birth, and good looks.[14] His answer is no, even though, as he surely knew, Socrates was deficient in almost all of these things. But, Aristotle thought, it is hard to say that a person who lacks these things has the same chance of living a successful life as a person who has them.

Although many people today would disagree, Aristotle was only reflecting the standards that were prevalent in his day. A person without the external goods he mentions would have been unlikely to lead armies into battle, erect public monuments at his own expense, or decide important matters of state. If those were the achievements people at that time thought mattered in life, why pretend that someone who could not accomplish them could be successful? No doubt, our own culture looks at things differently. But then, Aristotle would contend, it is our job to express the values *we* live by and the kinds of things *we* think separate a successful life from an unsuccessful one. Behind this approach is the conviction that it does no one any good to hold society to standards that are out of reach for all but a select few.

Along similar lines, Hegel rejected the idea that moral standards can be determined by rational thought independent of the practices of real people. He protested that morality cannot be a set of abstract principles imposed by philosophers on the rest of the population or even by a God issuing orders from heaven. Thus, the only way to investigate a society is to examine "the present and the actual, not the erection of a beyond supposed to exist, God knows where."[15]

To his point, it would be just as wrong to hold us to the standards of ancient Israelite society as it would be to hold ancient Israelite society to ours. Our ancestors accepted slavery and polygamy; we do not. We accept freedom of expression and religious toleration; they would not. In view of these differences, it would be folly to think that our understanding of terms like "freedom," "justice," or "democracy" would have made sense to them.

By this, Hegel did not mean that every society lives up to the standards it sets for itself. Some societies were failures even if judged by their own standards. Some made no contribution to what Hegel considered the march of history toward its final end: the achievement of human freedom. In fact, Hegel was not entirely satisfied with his own society.[16] His point was, it is wrong to hold any society to standards taken out of their cultural and historical context.

To take an obvious example, Hegel thought that the idea of a League of Nations that would secure perpetual peace was unrealistic.[17] Because there is no moral authority above individual states, if a conflict breaks out, the only way to settle it would be through war. To be sure, war in

Hegel's day was more contained and more humane than anything we have seen in the past 150 years; but it was war nonetheless. Should a political leader hold out for an ideal that has little chance of working or take the necessary action to protect the homeland? For many the answer is obvious.

The other side of the picture is occupied by Plato (ca. 428–347 BCE) and Kant (1724–1804). In one of his dialogues, Plato has a character say to Socrates that if he is serious about what he is arguing, then human life would have to be turned upside down because most people are doing the opposite of what they should do.[18] The answer is, of course, that Socrates was serious and that he pointed to a way of living well beyond anything his fellow Athenians could have imagined—a life that placed little if any importance on wealth, high birth, political power, or physical beauty. Socrates himself was fat, bald, snub-nosed, and had no appetite for political office.

In the eighteenth century, Kant sounded like a prophet himself when he said that to be legitimate, morality must be "stern, unindulgent, and truly commanding."[19] In other words, he thought that morality must impose the highest standards regardless of whether people actually live up to them. If lying is immoral, then, according to his way of thinking, it is always wrong to lie, even if one is telling a white lie or just trying to avoid an unpleasant social situation. To "indulge" in lying would be to rob the commandment "Though shall not lie" of its moral purity.

Kant would have acknowledged the existence of differences between ancient Israelite society and our own. His point was that, whatever the differences might be, and whatever social context we are in, it is still wrong to lie, oppress the poor, or use false weights and measures in the marketplace. In a nutshell, we cannot lower the standards of morality to bring them into conformity with human behavior as we observe it, because human behavior as we observe it leaves much to be desired.

Consider an example. The U.S. Constitution guarantees every citizen equal protection under the law. Although this is a worthy goal, it is doubtful whether the United States or any other country has ever lived up to it. Should we respond to this by saying that no country is perfect and therefore all we can do is proceed as we have been with mixed results, or should we say that the goal of equal protection is so important that we must keep it before our minds at all times? Kant comes down on the side of the latter. The fact that that no society in history has ever lived up to the standard of perfect justice is not a justification for modifying that standard.[20] History, as Heschel pointed out, and as Kant would agree, is a nightmare, the realm where greed and power hold sway.[21]

What worried Kant about lowering the standards of morality to take account of existing behavior was the prospect of society succumbing to moral backsliding. People with fewer scruples than Aristotle or Hegel might say, "Sure, there is cheating in the marketplace; but let's face it, that's how people are." In addition to being a dubious argument, this sentiment is likely to have more appeal to the cheaters than to their victims. Again, from Heschel: "Man must live on the summit to avoid the abyss."[22] The great Jewish Neo-Kantian Hermann Cohen (1842–1918) would amend this to say that man must *aim* for the summit to avoid the abyss. In other words, if we cannot attain perfect justice, we can strive for it in the hope that our efforts will give us something better than what we now have. Were we to give up the goal of perfect justice, not only would we not attain it, we would not even be moving in the right direction.

We do not have to probe very deeply to see that while Amos did not have Plato and Kant's theoretical sophistication, he was on their side — or, rather, they were on his side. We saw that when Amos says that God has singled out Israel of all the families of the earth (3:2), he follows it with: "That is why I will call you to account / For all your iniquities." Again, this implies that God expects more, not less, from Israel.[23] The fact that the nation has not yet lived up to the expectations God set for it does not show that these expectations are invalid. On the contrary, the expectations apply to every age and every place where Jews find themselves.

If this is right, then Amos would have resisted any suggestion that by insisting on justice for the poor, he was being unrealistic. If the society in which he lived failed to abide by the standards he put forth, then he was perfectly willing to say that his society was at fault and needed to alter its ways. As Kaufmann puts it, the prophets were religious and moral idealists who were deeply disappointed by the gulf that separated the ideal from reality.[24] Isaiah, for example, longed for the day when people would put more trust in the word of God than in horses and chariots (see chapter 3). All in all, the prophets believed that desperate measures were needed to correct existing conditions. In their own ways, then, Amos and Plato and Kant were disturbed by the prevailing attitudes of their era and looked forward to a time when humanity would undergo a moral and spiritual awakening that would set things right.

Still, the similarities between a prophet and two philosophers should not prevent us from recognizing the differences between them. Unlike the philosophers, Amos did not offer anything in the way of sustained argument. His technique for effectuating a moral and spiritual awakening was to shame his audience and force it to take a close look at itself. If that did not work, he appealed to the people's sense of self-preservation by warning of impending disaster.

Not only did Amos not offer sustained arguments; he never offered specific proposals for how to reform society. He never recommended abolishing the priesthood or the monarchy, nor did he call for organized resistance to the way either one was being administered. Add to this that he never displays any readiness to sit down at a table and work through concrete proposals.[25] To some, this exemplifies the whole problem with moral idealism: by insisting on absolute standards of right and wrong, it overlooks the possibility of making incremental change.

Rather than incremental change, Amos wanted substantial change. His mission was to call people's attention to the problem, convey God's utter displeasure with their behavior, and urge them to act before it is too late. He was successful to the degree that he called attention to the social ills that needed changing. Even today it is hard to read him without feeling a measure of the indignation he felt at the way people treated the poor. But he was not successful in effectuating the moral awakening he hoped for. The people ignored him and continued to act as they had before.

In modern parlance, Amos was a muckraker. Today, we might view him as the patron saint of all those who believe that religious observance must be combined with social action. Martin Luther King Jr., for one, quoted Amos in his famous "I Have a Dream" speech. For Amos, religion cannot be a closed environment where prayers are said and ceremonies enacted. The distinction we moderns generally make between secular and religious life would not have made sense to him. Nor did he set his sights on a mystical world far removed from this one. His message to us is all-encompassing and rooted in the present: a person who wants to serve God must be concerned with what is happening at this moment in this world, which is to say with schools, social welfare agencies, orphanages, prisons, law courts, marketplaces, and more. In the end, Amos's message is astonishingly simple: You cannot serve a just and merciful God unless you are just and merciful yourself.

CHAPTER 2

Hosea

Divine Pathos

My heart recoils within Me
My compassion grows warm and tender.
I will not execute my fierce anger.
I will not destroy Ephraim.

—HOSEA 11:8

Little is known about the life of Hosea except that he prophesized in the Northern Kingdom (called Ephraim) in the latter part of the eighth century BCE. This was a period of marked political instability: Four Israelite kings were assassinated in the span of fourteen years, and in 722 BCE the Assyrians conquered the kingdom. Like his older contemporary, Amos, Hosea was disgusted by the behavior he witnessed and predicted that God would exact punishment. But whereas Amos focused on social injustice, Hosea focused on idolatry.

What is idolatry and why is it often described in such dire terms? The Second Commandment prohibits two things: worshiping a god other than the God of Israel and depicting the God of Israel in material form. Although the prohibitions are clear, the reasons behind them are not. Why does God insist on being the only deity to be worshiped? Is it because the other gods do not exist or because the God of Israel is superior to the other gods? And if there are other gods beside the God of Israel, what is so terrible about acknowledging their presence? For example, couldn't we recognize other gods if we also affirm that the God of Israel is superior to them and the one to whom we owe a special allegiance?

Why, in addition, does God not want to be depicted in material form? Is it because God is not material and therefore cannot be drawn or sculpted, or because God does not want to be worshiped the way polytheistic gods are? If God can be seen, as Exodus 24:9 tells us and the prophets Isaiah (6:1) and Ezekiel (1:26–28) appear to affirm, then in principle wouldn't it be possible to create a likeness of God? And if we did create one, wouldn't it serve God's needs and ours if we bowed down to it?

The medieval philosophers tried to clear up these issues by saying that God is not material and that no other gods exist. For them, the sin of idolatry is an intellectual error: believing in something that does not exist and treating an immaterial being as if it were material. But keep in mind that they were heirs to a rich philosophic tradition that began in Greece and was deepened and broadened by Islamic thinkers in the Middle East. In biblical times, this tradition had not yet started. Biblical thinkers therefore had to develop their own understanding of why the Bible forbids idolatry. (That is why, like monotheism, the concept of idolatry evolved over time.[1]) To repeat: the Second Commandment tells us *that* idolatry is a sin but not *why*. This is the issue on which Hosea would stake his claim as a prophet.

Idolatry as Adultery — or Worse

Lacking the theoretical sophistication of the medieval philosophers, Hosea viewed idolatry as a moral failing. He therefore drew a connection between idolatry and adultery; in fact, not just adultery but whoredom — leaving one's spouse for lovers who pay for sexual favors and offer more money than the spouse can provide:

> I will go after my lovers,
> Who supply my bread and my water,
> My wool and my linen,
> My oil and my drink. (2:7)

In Hosea's mind, there is no more loathsome form of behavior. Just as a husband and a wife take a solemn vow on their wedding day, so Hosea contends, Israel took a solemn vow to remain loyal to God. According to Exodus 19:5, God said to Israel: "If you will obey Me faithfully and keep My covenant (*brit*), you shall be My treasured possession among all the peoples." Though Israel pledged itself to the covenant at Mount Sinai, Hosea charges that the nation has broken the covenant and gone whoring among the pagan gods of the land.[2]

Were things really this bad? It is difficult to know, because in ancient times "idolatry" could have involved a host of beliefs or practices such as magic, divination, necromancy, worship of local gods, or worship of the true God in material form or in high places. Kaufmann argues that rather than temples, priests, or formal mythologies devoted to other gods, the idolatry of the ancient Israelites consisted mainly of superstition, including the use of amulets, spells, special rites, or belief in satyrs and demons.[3]

Despite Kaufmann's claim, it is more likely that the ancient Israelites did worship foreign gods such as Baal and Asherah, because they were prominent in the area and gave the people tangible symbols on which to focus. It is hard to worship a God you cannot see or depict in material form. Since we do not have theological works from this period, we cannot say for sure what people thought. All we know is that Hosea found the people's behavior abhorrent and viewed it as a rejection of God.

It would be one thing if Hosea drew his analogy between idolatry and adultery in the abstract; what makes his message all the more poignant is that he lived it himself. When God first speaks to him, rather than saying "Take this message to the Israelites," God says, "Go, get yourself a wife of whoredom and children of whoredom, for the land will stray [play the whore] from following the LORD" (Hosea 1:2). Again, straying by worshiping other gods is compared to straying by having sex outside of marriage.

Generations of commentators have wondered whether God's command should be taken literally or figuratively. Was Hosea really supposed to marry a woman of ill-repute? According to Maimonides,

God never actually said this; the whole experience took place in the prophet's dream.[4] But Hosea's actions suggest that his interpretation of God's command was indeed literal: He married a woman named Gomer, who either was a prostitute at the time of the marriage or became one soon thereafter. She bore three illegitimate children, to whom Hosea gave ominous names: Jezreel [God will sow], No-Mercy, and Not My People.[5]

In ancient Israel, adultery was punishable by death. Thus Hosea would have been within his rights to seek retribution. At 2:4–5 he renounces Gomer, saying:

> Rebuke your mother, rebuke her–
> For she is not My wife
> And I am not her husband—
> And let her put away her harlotry from her face
> And her adultery from between her breasts.
> I will strip her naked
> And leave her as on the day she was born;
> And I will make her like a wilderness,
> Render her like desert land,
> And let her die of thirst.
> I will also disown her children;
> For they are now a harlot's brood.

The references to wilderness and a desert imply a strong connection between Gomer's infidelity to Hosea and Israel's infidelity to God. If the nation does not renounce its attachment to other gods and return to the true God, the land that once flowed with milk and honey will grow barren.

Hosea's prophecy would be much simpler, and for that reason much less interesting, if it ended here. Israel has gone astray. God has warned the nation to change its ways. If it does not, God's anger will be as intense as that of a husband whose wife sells her body to other men. The fact is, however, that Hosea's prophecy now goes into excruciating detail about the agony the husband feels over his wife's betrayal—and, by implication, that God feels over Israel's betrayal. On the one hand, there is outrage:

Now I will uncover her shame
In the very sight of her lovers,
And none shall save her from Me.
And I will end all her rejoicing:
Her festivals, new moons, and Sabbaths–
All her festive seasons.
I will lay waste her vines and her fig trees,
Which she thinks are a fee
She received from her lovers;
I will turn them into brushwood,
And beasts of the field will devour them. (2:10–12)

Later, the images become even more violent:

So I am become like a lion to them,
Like a leopard I lurk on the way;
Like a bear robbed of her young I attack them
And rip open the casing of their hearts;
And I will devour them there like a lion,
The beasts of the field shall mangle them. (13:7–8)

In subsequent verses, conflicting emotions are expressed in the space of a few lines. God has called Israel to service, freed it from bondage, offered sustenance in the desert, and led it to the Promised Land—and in return Israel has repaid God by getting in bed with foreign gods and exchanging sexual favors for cheap thrills![6] Despite such outrage, there is the love the husband feels for his wife and that God once felt, and at some level still feels, for Israel. Although we tend to think of love and hate as opposites, at times of crisis or disappointment, they often come together in a feeling of exasperation. Thwarted love can express itself as revulsion, rejection, revenge, or, almost inexplicably, once again as love. In this vein, amid the violence of a lion attacking its prey, Hosea proclaims (2:16–17):

Assuredly,
I will speak coaxingly to her
And lead her through the wilderness
And speak to her tenderly.
I will give her vineyards from there,
And the Valley of Achor as a plowland of hope.
There she shall respond as in the days of her youth,
When she came up from the land of Egypt.

And again at 11:8–9:

How can I give you up, O Ephraim?
How surrender you, O Israel?
How can I make you like Admah,
Render you like Zeboiim?[7]
I have had a change of heart,
All my tenderness is stirred.
I will not act on My wrath,
Will not turn to destroy Ephraim.
For I am God, not man.
The Holy One in your midst:
I will not come in fury.

Tenderness and rage are the two sides of God's response to Israel. In the end, tenderness wins out (2:20: "I will take you for my wife in faithfulness"), but there is a great deal of turmoil in the meantime.

While Hosea's account of God's response may not be a paragon of logical consistency, emotional outbursts rarely are. The question raised by his account is whether it is legitimate to describe God as suffering the agony of a jilted lover. Can the being who created heaven and earth, who wields limitless power and knows all things, feel the pangs of rejection? Can God feel exasperated enough to lose control and strike out in different directions? Or, is the whole idea that God feels emotion wrong from the start?

If we follow a literal reading of the Bible, God not only feels emotion, but does so with great intensity. At Exodus 32:10, God is so angry with the Israelite nation that God threatens to destroy it and start over. Only a desperate plea from Moses saves the day. Isaiah 30:27–28 tells us that God's anger burns so hot that God's lips are like a devouring fire. Isaiah 42:18 goes so far as to say that God will scream like a woman in labor. In addition to anger and anguish, we hear of sadness or regret (Gen. 6:6), jealousy (Exod. 20:5, 34:14), hate (Ps. 5:5, 11:5, Hosea 9:15), compassion (Gen. 19:16), love (Hosea 11:1), and joy (Isa. 62:5). How literally should we take these passages? Does God have lips or let out screams? Even if the answer is no, there is still the deeper question: Is there such a thing as divine pathos? In other words, can God be so affected by human action as to feel distress?

Heschel leaves no doubt about the answer: "An analysis of prophetic utterances shows that the fundamental experience of the prophet is a fellowship with the feelings of God, a *sympathy with the divine pathos*, a communion with the divine consciousness which comes about through the prophet's reflection of, or participation in, the divine pathos."[8] In other words, the prophet does not feel anguish alone. Rather, the prophet enters into a relationship with God to share these feelings. Building on this idea, Heschel maintains that God does not judge the world in a state of detachment; rather, God is moved and affected by what happens. If this is right, then God can feel joy or sorrow, pleasure or wrath.[9] Despite Heschel's assurance, the question of divine pathos has troubled people for centuries. Before making up our minds, let us consider the arguments pro and contra.

The God of the Philosophers

The claim that God cannot be subject to emotion originates with Aristotle and in the Jewish world finds its highest expression in the thought of Maimonides. We can begin to understand their view by recognizing that our word "pathos" is derived from the Greek word meaning to experience or to suffer, and easily lends itself to the adjective "pathetic."[10] Although some may describe a jilted lover as pathetic, this school of thought argues that it is highly objectionable to apply the word to God.

To carry this line of thinking a step further, note that we are often critical of politicians who resort to appeals to emotion in order to sway their audience. Such appeals typically play on fear, racial prejudice, or other anxieties and shun evidence or sustained argument. When this happens, the audience is put in a passive condition: It is being manipulated rather than informed. In this vein, emotion often stands in contrast to thought or considered judgment. To say that a person's emotions have gotten the best of him is to say that he has lost control of himself. To this school of thought, it is impossible to say the same thing of God.

The next step is to recognize that emotions are often fleeting and imply that the person who has them is subject to changes in mood. We saw that Hosea's rhetoric moves from anger to tenderness and back again. Even the most stable person cannot help but feel joy on some occasions and sadness on others. Jewish tradition recognizes that such changes are natural parts of the human condition. On Yom Kippur, we are supposed to afflict our souls with pangs of regret, while a few days later, on Sukkot, we are supposed to rejoice.

There is nothing unusual about changes of mood when we are talking about our own experience. But how, Aristotle asks, can a perfect being undergo this kind of change — or *any* change? If God is perfect and lacking in nothing, then any change would mean that God becomes better or worse as a result. Neither alternative makes sense. To be sure, the things *around* God change: People make decisions, new generations take the place of old, empires rise and fall. But as the eternal standard of right and wrong, God's insight and judgment remain constant.

Maimonides picks up on this line of thinking by agreeing that emotions cloud a person's judgment. He asks us to consider the example of a judge who must decide whether to grant leniency to a person found guilty of a crime.[11] In his opinion, this sort of judgment should be made by looking at legal precedents and examining the moral character of the criminal, not because the judge is suddenly moved by feelings of anger or compassion. Anger or compassion can be aroused by a speaker employing charged rhetoric, whether or not she is sincere. To suppose that God can be moved by these same feelings, that an impassioned plea can sway divine judgment or that God agonizes over decisions, is to take human shortcomings and ascribe them to God.

Furthermore, in Maimonides' view, the tendency to attribute human characteristics to God constitutes the essence of idolatry. If our ancestors sinned against the Second Commandment by worshiping figures made of wood and clay, then, in his opinion, we, their descendants, sin against it by thinking of God as a glorified human being who feels human emotions and faces human problems.

So certain is Maimonides of this point that he insists that everyone from children on up should be taught that God does not experience emotion and is not subject to change from one moment to the next.[12] For him, ascribing emotions to God is tantamount to rejecting everything that Judaism stands for. Another way to see Maimonides' point is to recognize that when we talk about emotions, we are talking about a plurality of feelings or responses that often follow each other in rapid succession: anger to joy to uncertainty to regret. Yet, Maimonides contends, Judaism teaches first and foremost that God is one. If so, how can God move from one state to another?

Maimonides has a simple explanation for those biblical passages that say that God is angry or jealous: "Know that if you consider the whole of the Torah and all the books of the prophets, you will find that the *expressions, wrath, anger, and jealousy,* are exclusively used with reference to *idolatry.*"[13] In other words, whenever the Bible says that God is angry, it is not talking about divine psychology but trying to warn us about the evils of worshiping false gods.

If this is so, why doesn't the Bible just say what it means? Maimonides has a simple answer to this as well: Unlike a philosophical work founded on abstract principles and intended for a highly sophisticated audience, the Bible tells a story intended for the widest possible audience. Though we would be right to demand literal and precise language in the former context, such a demand would be completely out of place in the latter. Suppose someone had told Shakespeare to drop his metaphors and say what he meant in simple terms. It doesn't take a literary scholar to see that, under those conditions, his plays and poems would lose much of their appeal.

The same is true of the Bible, which often uses metaphors or parables to make its point. As a result, when reading the Bible, we have to ask ourselves whether certain descriptions should be taken literally or figuratively.[14] For example, the declaration that God rescued Israel from Egyptian bondage with a mighty hand and an outstretched arm (Ps. 136:12) does not have to mean that God has appendages like a human being; in my view it is simply a metaphorical way of referring to God's awesome power. Similarly, the attestation that Noah walked with God at Genesis 6:9 does not have to mean that they strolled down a garden path together; to me it means that because Noah was righteous, he found favor with God.

For Maimonides, the same is true of passages that say that God experiences emotion. When the Bible says that God is angry, it does not mean that God has become annoyed, but that when the people turn to other gods, their behavior is intolerable. When God says "I am an impassioned [or jealous] God" (Exod. 20:5), the meaning is not that God is envious of Baal or Asherah, but that if you worship these gods, you have gone terribly wrong and cannot turn to the true God for help.[15] Roughly the same is true of mercy or compassion. According to Maimonides, these qualities are not intrinsic features of God that stand opposed to anger or jealousy but features of the world God has created.[16] In other words, if you examine nature closely, you will find that God has given every species the means to protect itself, gather food, and reproduce. It is with reference to such acts of generosity that Judaism speaks of God's mercy and compassion.

The upshot, says Maimonides, is that God does not swing from anger to joy or from vindictiveness to compassion. Nor does God have emotional outbursts similar to those of Zeus or Athena in Greek mythology. If we are to remain faithful to monotheism, Maimonides contends, we cannot take anthropomorphic descriptions of God at face value. Rather, we have to probe deeper and try to discern a message that is compatible with a God who cannot be seen and whose likeness cannot be captured in material form. Anything less, and we will not be worshiping God, but a figment of our imaginations.

The Case for Divine Pathos

As is often the case with disputes of this kind, the other side, in this case Heschel's side, has arguments in its favor as well. The most obvious one is that Maimonides has to pay a high price for such an austere conception of God: a being whose existence is necessary, whose perfection is absolute, who is unaffected by anything that happens on earth, and who therefore is not subject to change. The main problem with this view is that it understands God as being entirely self-contained. This conflicts with a famous midrash (*Sifre Deuteronomy*, 346) in which God says: "If you are My witnesses, then I am God . . . but if you are not my witnesses, then, as it were (*kivyachol*), I am not God." It is not that God will cease to exist if the people are not witnesses, but that God's plan for the world will not be complete so long as humans and God are estranged. Thus Heschel's point: God is moved and affected by what happens on earth, which implies that God can feel emotions like joy or sorrow.

Another problem with the philosophic conception of God has to do with love. Maimonides talks at length about our love for God in the *Guide of the Perplexed*, but he never talks about God's love for us. This means that, for Maimonides, our love for God is never reciprocated. One does not have to insist on a literal reading of every passage to point out that God's love for Israel is a central biblical theme. As we saw, despite God's anger over social injustice in the prophecy of Amos, God still maintains a special relationship with Israel ("But, I will not wholly wipe out / The House of Jacob—declares the LORD." [Amos 9:8]). Similarly, in the quotation that opens this chapter, Hosea proclaims that God will never forsake Ephraim: "My heart recoils within Me / My compassion grows warm and tender. / I will not execute my fierce anger. / I will not destroy Ephraim" (11:8).

Behind the defense of divine pathos lies a difference of opinion on how to understand perfection. According to the philosophic conception of God, divine perfection has little or nothing to do with personality. Personality is a distinctly human quality that cannot be ascribed to God without turning God into a glorified human being. By contrast, the prophetic view of God is that a being that does not exhibit some degree of personality—a being that cannot love or recoil when its love is spurned—is by that fact alone less than perfect. For a proponent of the prophetic view, those who deny personality in God are guilty of undermining divine perfection. However exalted God's knowledge and power, if God cannot feel any degree of love or hate, then God would lack the most important perfection a being can have. In fact, if this were true, humans, who can experience love or hate, would actually be superior to God.

The final step in the defense of divine pathos is to point out how much of religious liturgy consists in praise of God. We praise God for creating the world, freeing us from Egyptian bondage, endowing us with the Torah, and calling us to divine service. When Moses asks to see God's glory at Exodus 33, he is told that while no one can see God's face and live, God will cause all of the divine goodness to pass before him and "proclaim . . . the name LORD, and the grace that I grant and the compassion that I show." God then elaborates on this at Exodus 34, saying that God is compassionate, gracious, slow to anger, abounding in kindness and faithfulness, forgiving of sin, but not willing to clear the guilty.[17]

This, it can be argued, is one of the most important passages in the Torah because it sets forth what one might call the features of the divine persona. In this way, it reinforces the idea that God is concerned with what happens on earth and does have emotional responses to it. It is this God who experiences the torment of seeing Israel turn toward strange gods. It is this God who is worthy of the highest praise—for absent these features, we would be left with a God for whom such praise would be meaningless.

How should we reconcile these viewpoints? I think we can make progress if we take a closer look at what we mean by anger, mercy, love, and compassion. Consider anger. There is the anger that comes with losing one's temper, the kind that causes blood pressure to rise, the heart to race, and the mind to stop thinking clearly. This kind of anger often leads to violence or other forms of antisocial behavior. But there is also the kind of anger that comes with seeing someone take advantage of someone else. So far from compromising rational thought, the second kind of anger might be said to be paradigmatic of it, because it is a legitimate reaction to moral outrage. Any morally sensitive person should be disturbed when she sees someone taking advantage of someone else. It was this kind of disturbance that made Amos criticize the people of the Northern Kingdom. Rather than calling this kind of disturbance *anger*, then, let us call it righteous indignation. We might well conclude that a being who cannot experience such indignation would not qualify as a moral agent.

Similar considerations apply to mercy. There is the mercy one feels after listening to an impassioned speech and the mercy one feels after hearing a guilty person express remorse. Most people can give an impassioned speech or utter the words "I'm sorry." By contrast, sincere remorse tells us something important about the character of the person who expresses it: The person has accepted responsibility for his actions and will try not to repeat them. As with anger, one response bypasses rational thought, while the other presupposes it.

Moving to love, there is a response based on physical attraction and a response based on affection and admiration. There is compassion based on family or neighborhood affiliation and compassion based on the fact that another person has suffered a misfortune. To be sure, these differences are not always easy to identify, and, in some cases, both reactions may be present. Nonetheless, in my view, we have to take these differences into consideration if we are to resolve the question before us.

Of course, God cannot feel emotion if that means losing control, being swayed by charged rhetoric, or experiencing physical attraction. Heschel comes close to admitting this when he says that the prophets did not conceive of God's pathos "as a sort of fever of the mind which, disregarding the standards of justice, culminates in irrational and irresponsible action."[18] If so, then the pathos we are talking about is not the normal kind. It does not imply that God can be pathetic or that God undergoes changes of mood in the way humans do.[19]

The crux of divine pathos is the recognition that God is a moral agent who approves of some things and disapproves of others. There are people whose repentance is sincere and people whose repentance is phony, people who should be given a second chance in life and people for whom some form of punishment is indicated. If God is the ultimate judge of such things, then there are times when God's judgment is to grant mercy and times when it is to insist on justice. This does not mean that God swings back and forth between them, but that in any given case, certain factors need to be taken into account before a final decision is reached.

According to this way of thinking, Amos was perfectly justified in saying that God abhors abuse of the poor. This does not mean that God gets angry in the way we do, but that in God's judgment, abuse of the poor is wrong and must stop. Similarly, Hosea was justified in comparing God to a faithful spouse and Israel to an unfaithful one. This does not mean that God experiences a conflict between love and hate, but that however egregious Israel's infidelity may be at any given point, God's promise to redeem it remains intact.

In this way, we can side with Maimonides and the philosophic tradition when it says that God does not undergo change. Abuse of the poor was wrong in the past, is wrong now, and will remain wrong as long as people inhabit the earth. Likewise, the promise of redemption remains in place no matter how much we may disregard it. These judgments constitute the bedrock of the prophetic view of the world. But we can also side with Heschel when he says that God is concerned with what we do. None of this implies that God agonizes over judgments or suffers anguish. Rather, it implies that the qualities revealed to Moses in

Exodus 34 are legitimate: God is gracious, slow to anger, and abounding in faithfulness, but will exact punishment when the person merits it.

A Recourse to Anthropomorphism

Like Amos, Hosea was a prophet rather than a systematic thinker. From a moral standpoint, he was pointing out the harm done when a person — or, in this case, an entire nation — breaks a promise. As with Hosea and Gomer, or God and Israel, this is not just any promise, but a marriage vow, which is to say an expression of love. The sin involved is terrible — and thereby Hosea uses every rhetorical device at his disposal to make his point. That is why we hear God threatening to attack Israel with all the ferocity of a lion attacking its prey and to lay waste of all its vines and end all of its rejoicing. But in the end, mercy overrides justice — and that is why we also hear that God is anxious to take Israel back and looks forward to the day when Israel will reaffirm its marriage vow.

There is in all of this a fair measure of anthropomorphism. It is hard to imagine how Hosea could have captured the attention of his listeners or readers otherwise. If we were to compare the impact of his message to that of even the most articulate philosopher, who would doubt that the philosopher would suffer by comparison? Even so, systematic thought has a role to play. The comparison between Hosea's anguish and God's rests on an analogy, and like all analogies, it can take us only so far. We are not being asked to shed tears for God in the way we might for Hosea. Rather, we are being asked to take action. Consider Hosea 14:2:

Return, O Israel, to the LORD your God, . . .
Say to Him:
"Forgive all guilt
And accept what is good."

If Israel will abandon its immoral ways, reaffirm the covenant, and accept what is good, all the anguish and threats of destruction will be forgotten. This is another way of saying that the prophets' anthropomorphic descriptions of God were not aimed at advancing a theory to rival that of the great philosophers—people of whom Hosea and his contemporaries knew nothing—but to bring about a practical result: reconciliation between God and Israel. To the degree that Hosea's exhortation hastens that result, it does exactly what its author intended.

CHAPTER 3

First Isaiah, Part 1

War and Peace

In the days to come,
The Mount of the LORD's House
Shall stand firm above the mountains
And tower over the hills;
And all the nations Shall gaze on it with joy.
And the many peoples shall go and say:
"Come,
Let us go up to the Mount of the LORD,
To the House of the God of Jacob;
That he may instruct us in his ways,
And that we may walk in His paths."
For instruction shall come forth from Zion,
The word of the LORD from Jerusalem.
Thus he will judge among the nations
And arbitrate for the many peoples,
And they shall beat their swords into plowshares
And their spears into pruning hooks:
Nation shall not take up
Sword against nation;
They shall never again know war.

—ISAIAH 2:3–4

Although the book of Isaiah goes under the name of a single prophet, it is generally agreed that it contains the writings of three people. The first occupies chapters 1–39, the second 40–55, and the third 56–66.[1] This chapter and the next one will take up the thought of the First Isaiah (or simply Isaiah for short), whose ministry took place in the Southern Kingdom (Judah) during the end of the eighth century BCE.

Isaiah's Political Prophesies

Isaiah prophesied for approximately four decades, which took him through the reigns of Kings Uzziah, Jotham, Ahaz, and Hezekiah. The period in question extends from the eighth to the early seventh century BCE. As kings go, this group was a mixed lot, with some successful rulers and some regrettable ones. Although Uzziah extended the boundaries of the kingdom and ushered in a period of prosperity, he grew proud, appropriated some of the ritual duties reserved for the priests, and eventually was stricken with leprosy. Jotham, who reigned as a co-regent when his father was suffering from leprosy, continued to expand the kingdom and to sustain its prosperity. Jotham's son Ahaz was forced to confront the growing power of Assyria, which meant that he had to choose between joining an anti-Assyrian alliance or becoming an Assyrian vassal state. He chose the latter, fought a costly war against the alliance, and became so pro-Assyrian that he erected a Syrian altar in the Jerusalem Temple. The Bible (2 Kings 16:3–4) also records that he engaged in abominable practices such as human sacrifice.

The last king, Hezekiah, removed the idols from the Temple and restored traditional religious practices but continued to pay tribute to Assyria until the Assyrian king Sargon II was killed in battle. At that point, Hezekiah tried to enlist first Babylonian and then Egyptian support to form another anti-Assyrian alliance. Angered by Hezekiah's actions, Sargon's successor, Sennacherib, attacked Judah and came close to destroying it. In an effort to appease Sennacherib, Hezekiah paid a lavish tribute, including gold from the doors and doorposts of the Temple (2 Kings 18:13–15). Apparently this was not enough, and Sennacherib attacked again. The Bible (2 Kings 19:35) says that Jerusalem was spared when an angel smote the Assyrian army as it was laying siege to the city. Another account holds that Hezekiah closed off all the sources of fresh water, forcing the Assyrian army to drink contaminated water, which led to an outbreak of cholera.[2]

Sandwiched between major powers like Egypt and Assyria, the small state of Judah faced the problem of how to preserve its ethnic and religious identity, not to mention its very existence. After all, oppose a major power and you confront the prospect of annihilation. Recall that when the Assyrians conquered the Northern Kingdom in 722 BCE, the people were sent into exile, never to be heard from again. On the other hand, Judah's alternative—becoming a vassal state—could be just as risky. In addition to fighting battles in defense of the dominant state, a vassal state had to levy taxes on its citizens to pay tribute. Worse, there was always the possibility that the dominant state might demand that the vassal state honor its gods by erecting statues of those gods in public places and adopting the dominant state's religious practices.

What, then, was a small state like Judah supposed to do? It was all very well to hold out the ideal of peace, as Isaiah did in the verses beginning this chapter, but how was one supposed to get there?

Isaiah's Answer

Immersing himself in the political issues of the day, in particular how to deal with the grim reality of military might, Isaiah rails against the nation's alliances with foreign rulers and any policy that asked the people to put their trust in weapons. For example, during the Syro-Ephraimite War of 734–33 BCE, Syria and the Northern Kingdom attacked Judah because Judah had refused to join their coalition. According to 2 Chronicles 28:1–8, 120,000 Judean soldiers were slaughtered in a single day, several high-ranking officials including King Ahaz's son were killed, and 200,000 women and children were exiled to the North.[3] What advice does Isaiah give amid this crisis? "Be firm and be calm. Do not be afraid and do not lose heart" (7:3).

Be calm? Isaiah assures Ahaz that his enemies will fail, which turned out to be true in the end. But instead of putting his trust in God, Ahaz turned to Assyria for help, a tragic decision in Isaiah's opinion. It is at this point that Isaiah prophesies that a son named Immanuel will be born to a young woman and that by the time the son can tell the difference between good and bad, the people will be eating curds and honey and the nations plotting against Judah will be destroyed. We saw that this sign was ambiguous and, according to most accounts, could not be verified for years to come. With enemies attacking his country at that moment, how could Ahaz remain calm?

Isaiah went on to predict that, as punishment for Ahaz's lack of faith, Assyria would turn against Judah and only a small remnant of the Judean nation would survive. In fact, by 10:5, he claims that Assyria will do God's work ("Rod of My anger") by punishing Judah, after which Assyria, a proud and arrogant nation that does not recognize God, will be punished itself. Eventually, the Davidic dynasty would be restored, followed by an era of peace. In Isaiah's eyes, then, the crisis in which Ahaz and Judea were enmeshed was part of a divine plan that would radically transform the political map of the ancient Near East.

In addition to his oracle foretelling the destruction of Assyria, Isaiah issues oracles against Babylonia, Egypt, Philistia, Moab, and Syria. The lesson to be learned is that no nation, no matter how powerful, can shield itself from divine judgment. In fact, in a passage that has come to be known as the "Isaiah Apocalypse" (24–27), he proclaims that God's final judgment will encompass the whole earth:

> Behold,
> The LORD will strip the earth bare,
> And lay it waste,
> And twist its surface,
> And scatter its inhabitants. . . .
> The earth shall be bare, bare;
> It shall be plundered, plundered,
> For it is the LORD who spoke this word. (24:1–3)

If God created the heavens and the earth in a single moment, Isaiah is saying, they could be destroyed just as easily. Or, if the nation put its trust in God, it will be protected from its enemies and enjoy all the benefits of peace. This whole way of looking at things is what Buber calls "theopolitics."[4] Behind the theopolitics of the prophets is a God-centered view of history. God, entangled in the affairs of nations, will see to it that however dismal things may seem at present, justice will prevail in the end. But again, what was the ruler of a nation who had to make day-to-day decisions to protect his people supposed to do?

Although Hezekiah trusted in God and found favor with God (2 Kings 18:3–8), he was also a practical man who made weapons, repaired the walls of Jerusalem, and built a tunnel to carry water into the city so that it could hold out against a siege. When he considers joining an alliance with Egypt to help fend off Syria, Isaiah becomes infuriated. An alliance with Egypt? After all, God had liberated the Jewish people from Egypt. Now, instead of renewing their covenant with God, they are seeking to enter into one with Pharaoh.

> Oh, disloyal sons!
> —declares the LORD—
> Making plans
> Against my wishes,
> Weaving schemes
> Against my will,
> Thereby piling
> Guilt on guilt—
> Who set out to go down to Egypt
> Without asking Me,
> To seek refuge with Pharaoh,
> To seek shelter under the protection of Egypt. (30:1–2)

In addition, Isaiah lambasts the nation's folly of putting trust in horses and chariots rather than the word of God. As he proclaims at 31:3: "Their horses are flesh, not spirit." In our day, Isaiah's advice could easily be shifted to tanks, which are metal, not spirit. If Assyria falls, Isaiah assures the people (31:8), it will not be by the sword of man.

When it comes to specific advice, Isaiah reiterates what he said earlier to Ahaz:

> For thus said my LORD God,
> The Holy One of Israel,
> "You shall triumph by stillness and quiet;
> Your victory shall come about
> Through calm and confidence." (30:15)

With an enemy at the gate, Isaiah again asks for calm, promising that God will protect the nation better than any earthly power. In this context the prophet Zechariah (4:6) comes to mind: "Not by might, nor by power, but by My Spirit—said the LORD of Hosts." Yet, again, where is the ruler willing to trust in spirit? How long would he last if he did?

Theopolitics versus Realpolitik

The Bible is not the only ancient source to raise these questions. In his *History of the Peloponnesian War*, the ancient Greek historian Thucydides recounts the story of Athens sending ambassadors to the tiny island of Melos to ask the inhabitants to pay tribute.[5] When the Melians refuse, the Athenians point out that the way of the world is that the strong do what they want and the weak suffer what they must. In other words, in international relations, only one thing matters: raw power. When the Melians invoke considerations of fairness and morality, the Athenians scoff. Justice, they counter, is nothing more than political expediency. "Why trust in the future," they ask, "more than what is currently in front of your eyes?" Still, the Melians refuse to pay tribute, after which the Athenians slaughter every male on the island and sell the women and children into slavery.

Such is the conflict between Buber's "theopolitics" and what is commonly called "realpolitik."[6] One is based on faith in a just and merciful God, the other on the exercise of power. One calls for a steadied calm, the other for immediate action. One appeals to our better nature, the other to our instinct for survival.

Against Buber, Walzer argues that theopolitics is really a withdrawal from politics as we normally understand it.[7] When Isaiah tells kings to be calm, he is asking them to reject alliances with other nations and trust in God. Imagine if someone had given this advice to Churchill or Roosevelt in World War II, when the issue of joining an alliance with Stalin was raised. Does anyone really think that Nazi Germany could have been defeated had they turned their backs on Stalin and turned to God for help?

God and History

This is another way of asking what role God plays in the history of national conflicts. Heschel characterizes Isaiah's view of history as follows: "The world's great powers are instruments of the divine will. Not the elements of nature, but primarily the powers of history carry out the designs of God."[8] As a historical claim about Isaiah's worldview, this is undoubtedly correct. The prophets did not recognize nature as a force of its own. According to Isaiah, even a foreign nation like Assyria could play a role in God's governance of the world. (Later prophets such as Jeremiah and Ezekiel would even see the hand of God in the destruction of the Temple.) After the present dangers have passed, Isaiah foresees a time when the Davidic dynasty will be restored, the world will turn to Jerusalem for guidance, and peace will reign. "Like the birds that fly, even so will the LORD of Hosts shield Jerusalem, shielding and saving, protecting and rescuing" (31:5).

To be sure, there are cases where, unbeknown to them, agents who pursue evil wind up producing God's desired end. After Joseph reveals himself to his brothers, he tells them not to be angry or distressed because it was God's will that he go to Egypt to save lives and fulfill the promise God had made to Abraham (Gen. 45). As bad as it was, the brothers' decision to sell him into slavery and lie to their father led to a noble end. Hegel based a whole theory on the idea that the people who make history may have little or no understanding of the consequences of their actions. What he termed the "cunning of reason" is the tendency for agents to act for personal or selfish motives but, due to the presence of unintended consequences, wind up ensuring that history proceeds according to a rational plan. For him, history is the story of ever-increasing manifestations of human freedom.

Hegel's reading of history was centered on Europe. He was most interested in such events as the fall of the Greek city-state, the rise of feudalism, and the French Revolution. Generally he ignored battles (e.g., the Bourbons versus the Hapsburgs) or whole countries (e.g., India) that did not accord with his worldview.

The problem is, as Heschel himself comes to admit, history does not proceed according to a well-orchestrated plan but is rather a nightmare. Hypocrisy, corruption, conflict, and oppression abound. How, then, can history be the arena in which God's designs are carried out? Was it God's design that eventually Jerusalem would fall to the Babylonians, that the Romans would destroy it twice over, that Christians and Muslims would fight a series of bloody battles there, or that Hitler would destroy virtually all of European Jewry? Was Rome—or, perish the thought, the ss—the rod of God's anger? Distasteful as these questions are, they have to be asked. Some Jews think the answer to these questions is yes. When the full extent of the Holocaust became known, some argued that God wanted Hitler to punish European Jews for their assimilationist tendencies. Even today, some argue that the Holocaust was the "price" Jews had to pay for the formation of the State of Israel.

To me, such responses, which have God in league with Hitler, are nothing but blasphemy. What kind of God would use unspeakable evil to teach people a lesson? What kind of end could compensate for 6,000,000 lives, including 1,500,000 children? Even if the Holocaust led to a millennium of world peace (which clearly has not happened), how could it be alleged that *we* are better off because *they* perished in the gas chambers? Given such monstrous evils, the whole idea of compensation is grotesque. To view every historical occurrence as part of an overarching divine plan would make God complicit in the most despicable forms of behavior and, in my view, undermine any possibility of thinking of

God as gracious, compassionate, and slow to anger. So far from being worthy of worship, such a God would arguably be worthy of contempt.

If, however, we reject the idea that every historical event reflects God's judgment, what becomes of Isaiah's view of history? Part of the answer is staring us in the face. The prophets did not hold back when it came to motivating people to change their ways. Their descriptions are graphic, their oracles gut-wrenching. Within the space of a few chapters, one is likely to find inspired poetry, condemnation of current practices, visions of apocalypse, and promises of redemption. How much of this is to be taken literally? Did Isaiah really think that carnivorous animals like wolves or leopards would lie down in perfect harmony with their prey—or was he trying to say that nations might one day live together in peace? Although no one knows for sure, I suspect it is the latter.

Another part of the answer requires us to accept Isaiah's limitations as a prophet trying to forecast future events. There is no way he could have foreseen Roman domination of the Mediterranean, the Crusades, the horrifying events of the twentieth century, or the rise of religious terrorism in our own century. Nor could he have anticipated countless other massacres that have occurred since ancient times. If history is a nightmare, then, as one of James Joyce's characters put it, it is a nightmare from which we are trying to awake. We do not know, and cannot speak with any certainty, as to what Isaiah might have said had he lived through these other events. Furthermore, whenever we aim to consider God's role in history, we have to keep in mind the limited nature of our understanding. As Second Isaiah (55:9) says:

> But as the heavens are high above the earth,
> So are My ways high above your ways
> And My plans above your plans.

Similarly, we saw that when Moses was alone with God on the mountain, God told him that no mortal can see the divine face and live.⁹ This is generally taken to mean that an aspect of God will always remain mysterious to us. If so, then anyone who claims to know exactly what God is or what God is thinking—including a prophet—is on shaky ground. As we will see when we get to the book of Job, the same is true of someone who claims to know how God's power is manifested in the world. The Bible tells us that God created heaven and earth, but the precise way in which God exercises power over them is unknown to even the wisest among us. When it comes to this aspect of divinity, all one can do is respond, as Job does, with wonder coupled with a deep sense of humility.

To continue with Moses and God, earlier we saw that God reveals the divine self as gracious, compassionate, and slow to anger. While these qualities may not tell us everything there is to know about God, they are the best that we in our limited knowledge can say. According to the prophets, too, as angry as God gets at the evils we perpetrate, graciousness and compassion win out in the end. If, however, we take away God's compassionate side, if the world is no longer ruled by a just and merciful creator, then it seems that the biblical conception of God loses all meaning. One might just as well worship a malevolent God—or no God at all.

The Value of Isaiah's Message

Can we then relinquish the idea that every agent in history is an instrument of the divine will and still find something of value in Isaiah's message? I think the answer is yes if we can pivot from the eighth century BCE to the twentieth century CE. The French philosopher Emmanuel Levinas (1906–95) wrote that the distinguishing feature of Jewish existence is its ability to stand apart from history and be its judge.[10] He meant that history is not always on the side of right: Sometimes bad causes triumph and the good ones are trampled on. The fact that the Temple was destroyed and the Jewish people scattered does not mean that the principles they stood for were refuted. The same goes for the countless pogroms and persecutions that followed. For Levinas, what distinguishes Judaism is its ability to exist *in defiance* of history. In other words, raw power is not the only way to settle problems. However uncommon it may be, a nation can put morality ahead of political expediency.

This, I believe, is what Isaiah wanted when he asked Hezekiah not to trust in horses and chariots. Those may not have been the best options from the standpoint of expediency. But if expediency is all we have, if no regard is paid to what Isaiah calls *spirit*, then he is telling us that whatever victory we achieve is likely to be fleeting.

In its day, Assyria was a mighty power that threatened everyone in its path, but it was conquered by Babylonia, which was conquered by Persia, which was conquered by Alexander the Great, much of whose empire was conquered by the Romans. In defiance of this, Isaiah looked forward to the day when nations would live together in peace. Although we are still waiting for that day to arrive, it is significant that Isaiah's vision captures our attention long after the Assyrian army has been forgotten. As discussed in chapter 2, the prophets were moral idealists. It is in that light that we should understand Isaiah's vision of lasting peace.

Taking Isaiah's lesson to heart may mean that we have to alter our conception of how God enters our lives. Given the historical record as we have it, it seems highly unlikely that God acts like a stage manager who puts everything in place and makes sure the actors follow a tight script. Nor is it likely that nothing can happen without God's approval. Rather, we might think of God as the commanding voice of morality. Such a voice puts before us a choice and asks us to follow our better nature—to live according to the teachings revealed at Sinai.

As Isaiah explains, this is what God wants of us:

> Cease to do evil;
> Learn to do good.
> Devote yourselves to justice;
> Aid the wronged.
> Uphold the rights of the orphan;
> Defend the cause of the widow. (1:16–17)

Not everyone hears this voice, and many of those who do choose to ignore it. Isaiah knew that—and still spoke of a day when swords would be beaten into plowshares. Here, as discussed earlier, we might take these words more as an exhortation than a prediction. It is not that peace will break out no matter what people do, so that we can keep to business as usual and let God do the necessary work. It is instead that peace will break out and Israel will become a light unto the nations *if* its people do what they promised to do when they entered into the covenant with God. If Isaiah is right, being a light unto the nations means that, to some extent, we all have to take up the cause of idealism.

What Makes Life Worth Living

From the standpoint of ordinary people, it often seems as if the prophets inhabit a different world than the rest of us. Whereas we tend to think in terms of what is going to happen tomorrow, they think in terms of what will happen when justice is finally served. Whereas we tend to focus on the necessities of everyday life, they focus on the ideals to which life should be committed. One of the challenges we face in reading them is how to balance these perspectives. No nation can safely avoid alliances with other nations. By the same token, Isaiah is telling us, no nation should think that alliances alone—or anything that falls under the rubric of political expediency—will be enough to secure the welfare of its people. In addition to survival, there is also the question of what we are surviving *for*.

It is at this point that Isaiah's urging that we devote ourselves to justice, aid the wronged, uphold the rights of the orphan, and defend the cause of the widow has real force. Although Isaiah lived more than 2,500 years ago, these demands are timeless in their application. The people, and that includes us today, have to listen to that part of their nature that recoils against oppression and feels compassion for the poor—that part that brings us closest to the God we have committed ourselves to follow. If we cannot accept everything Isaiah says about the way God acts in history, we can accept the claim that history will only become tolerable if we dedicate ourselves to the goals that Isaiah and the other prophets insist on. In place of war, peace; in place of hostility, compassion; in place of anger, composure. These are the qualities that make life worth living. If kings or rulers lose sight of them, however successful they may otherwise be in subduing their enemies, we must still regard them as failures.

CHAPTER 4

First Isaiah, Part 2

The Coming of the Messiah

A shoot shall come forth from the stump of Jesse.
A twig shall sprout from his stock.
The spirit of the LORD shall alight upon him:
A spirit of wisdom and insight,
A spirit of counsel and valor,
A spirit of devotion and reverence for the LORD.
He shall sense the truth by his reverence for the LORD:
He shall not judge by what his eyes behold,
Nor decide by what his ears perceive.
Thus he shall judge the poor with equity
And decide with justice for the lowly of the land.

—ISAIAH 11:1

The larger passage from Isaiah (excerpted here) is significant in predicting the coming of a messianic future: The Southern Kingdom of Judah will be ruled by a descendant of Jesse, David's father.[1] This will fulfill God's promise to David: "Your house and your kingdom shall ever be secure before you; your throne shall be established forever" (2 Sam. 7). And, unlike other kings, this one will rule with wisdom and understanding, bringing justice to the poor.

Although the Torah never explicitly mentions a Messiah, the idea that a descendant of David would usher in a new age came to play a major role in both Judaism and Christianity. The *Amidah* prayer, which traditional Jews recite three times a day, asks God to rebuild Jerusalem and establish within it the throne of David. Similar sentiments are expressed after reciting the haftarah and the Grace after Meals. In Christianity, the Gospel according to Matthew begins with an elaborate genealogy linking Jesus with the House of David and proclaims him the Messiah.

In the Middle Ages, Maimonides left no doubt about the importance of belief in the coming of the Messiah for Judaism: "King Messiah will arise and restore the kingdom of David to its former state and original sovereignty. . . . He who does not believe in a restoration or does not wait the coming of the Messiah denies not only the teachings of the prophets but also those of the Law of Moses our Teacher."[2] Maimonides also included belief in the coming of the Messiah as the twelfth of his Thirteen Principles of Faith, whose acceptance, he held, was necessary for any Jew to be worthy of salvation. In a later age, facing unspeakable horrors, Jews in ghettos and concentration camps would go to their deaths with Maimonides' words on their lips: "I believe with perfect faith in the coming of the Messiah, and though he may tarry, yet I believe."[3]

Judaism and Christianity may differ on who is the Messiah, what he will do, and how we can prepare for his coming, but they agree on at least this much: The way things are now is not the way they have to be or the way they will be in the future. This is another way of saying that the human condition is not tragic; however formidable life's difficulties may be at present, the forces of evil will not win out in the end.

A word of caution. In our day, we tend to think of the future as totally disconnected from the past—a time when political and technological progress will transform human life to such an extent that it will be almost unrecognizable to those who went before it. But this is not the way our ancient and medieval ancestors saw things. To them, the future would be a better time in large part because it would restore lost features of the past: reestablishing the Davidic dynasty, rebuilding Jerusalem, reaffirming the Sinai covenant. Along these lines, Maimonides thought that the Messiah would restore sovereignty to Israel so that the nation could go back to fulfilling all the commandments of the Torah. In effect, what *will be* is really a matter of what *should have been* all along.

As we have seen, Isaiah was not the first prophet to articulate such a vision. Amos talks about a time when God will rebuild Israel so that "they shall plant vineyards and drink their wine" (9:14). Hosea tells us that eventually the Israelites will seek God (3:5) and that God will take them back in love (14:5). Both mention David in their visions of return, but given that they spoke to the people of the Northern Kingdom, and the Davidic dynasty ruled in the South, these passages are often thought to be later additions. Jeremiah, who lived before the fall of Jerusalem, proclaims that God will make a new covenant with Israel and no longer remember their sins (31:31–34). Zechariah, who lived after the fall of Jerusalem, asserts that a triumphant and victorious king will enter Jerusalem but be so humble that he will ride a donkey (9:9).

Although Isaiah does not use the word *Mashiah* (Messiah), its etymology is not hard to discern. Originally *Mashiah* referred to someone who had been anointed with oil. In ancient Israel, kings and priests were anointed with oil as part of their installation ceremonies. Thus God tells Moses to anoint Aaron and his sons with oil (Exod. 30:30). Saul, David, and Solomon were anointed as well (1 Sam. 10:1, 16:13; 1 Kings 1:34–39). And the prophet Third Isaiah (61:1) said that God had anointed him to raise up the brokenhearted and proclaim liberty to the captives.

Eventually, the future redeemer promised by Amos, Hosea, and First Isaiah, the king who would usher in a whole new age, came to be known as the Messiah, or "anointed one of God." Hope for a time when oppression and injustice would vanish rested on the basis of this vision. When the Hebrew Bible was translated into Greek, *Mashiah* was rendered as *Christos* (Christ). In this way, Christians came to believe that Jesus was the fulfillment of God's promise of ultimate redemption.

Whether one is a Jew or Christian, the importance of redemption cannot be overemphasized. To see why, one has only to recognize that the Bible does not paint a rosy picture of human behavior. The first act that Adam and Eve take in the Garden of Eden is to defy God. The next thing we hear is that Cain was jealous of his brother Abel and killed him. Eventually there is so much evil in the world that God has to wipe out most of humanity by bringing a flood. But even the flood doesn't solve the problem, because shortly after Noah leaves the ark, Ham, his youngest son, commits some sort of atrocity against his father (Gen. 9:22). Joseph's brothers sell him into slavery and lie to their father about his death.

One might think that after God rescues Israel from Egyptian bondage, the picture would change, but that is hardly the case. Throughout the story of the Exodus, the people complain to Moses about lack of food and water, worship the Golden Calf, plead to be taken back to Egypt, and refuse to fight for their freedom. By Numbers 14, God becomes so angry with the people that they must wander in the desert until they die rather than enter the Promised Land. When Moses addresses the new generation in Deuteronomy, the generation that *will* enter the Promised Land, the picture still hasn't changed. Shortly before Moses' death (Deut. 31:16–18), God tells Moses in language similar to that used by Hosea that the new generation won't be any better than the old one and will go whoring after other gods.

We have seen that Amos, Hosea, and Isaiah are sharply critical of the people's behavior and warn that God is about to inflict punishment of terrifying proportions. This theme will reach its climax in Jeremiah, whose name (jeremiad) has become synonymous with a mournful complaint or recitation of woes. If these passages were all we had, reading the Bible would leave us in a state of despair. Why work to improve things if failure is inevitable? Or, to put the point another way, if the generation of the Exodus, who witnessed the miracle at the Red Sea and heard God's voice at Sinai, rebelled against God, what chance do we have of doing any better?

Fortunately, these passages are not all we have, because the prophets assure us that sin and rebellion against God are not the end of the story. The promise of a Messiah means that however bad a nightmare, history does not have to repeat itself. The end of the story will occur when a new type of leader appears, one who is able to do what Moses and the rest of the prophets could not—bring about reconciliation between God and

Israel. This is a bold claim, because it says that we should put aside the historical record and focus on something that has not yet happened. As God tells Second Isaiah (43:18–19): "Do not recall what happened of old, / Or ponder what happened of yore! / I am about to do something new."

Needless to say, waiting for something new to happen carries risks. If the Messiah has not come in all this time, how realistic is it to keep looking forward to his arrival? Yet, risky as it is, the hope for a new and better age has sustained the Jewish people through the destruction of two Temples, thousands of years of homelessness, the Spanish Inquisition, countless pogroms, even the horrors of the gas chambers, because it gives us reason to think that, as awful as things are now, evil will not triumph in the end.

Hope as a Moral Principle

Behind the idea of a messianic future is an important principle: Unless the future offers some prospect of improvement, there would be no reason to work to make things better. The result would be a grudging acceptance of the way things are at present. From what we have seen, this attitude would contradict everything the prophets stand for because it would mean making peace with corruption and rejection of God. In short, hope for a better future goes hand in hand with a call to action.

Yet, for all its importance, hope for a better future raises problems. "There is something grand about living in hope," wrote Gershom Scholem, "but at the same time there is something profoundly unreal about it."[4] The history of Judaism is littered with false hopes, false messiahs, as well as wild speculation about the circumstances in which the true Messiah will appear. In the ancient world there was Simon Bar Kokhba (who is discussed below). After him came Moses of Crete in the fifth century CE, Shabbatai Zevi in the seventeenth century, Jacob Frank in the eighteenth century, and by some accounts Menachem Mendel Schneerson in the twentieth century. Christianity has faced the same problem in connection with the Second Coming of Jesus. Although hope is needed when things get difficult, it is precisely when things get difficult that people are most susceptible to folly.

We can further appreciate the significance of this problem by looking at attempts to free Israel from the heavy hand of Roman domination. Two armed revolts occurred, one from 66 to 73 CE, and the other from 132 to 136 CE. With regard to the first, Josephus, our chief historical source for this period, writes: "Their chief inducement to go to war was an equivocal oracle also found in their [Jewish] sacred writings, announcing that at that time a man from their own country would become Monarch of the world. This they took to mean the triumph of their own race, and many of their own scholars were wildly out in their interpretations."[5]

The first Jewish revolt led to the destruction of the Second Temple as well as much of Jerusalem, civil war between competing Jewish factions, numerous massacres and crucifixions, and a large number of people being taken away as slaves. The second revolt was led by Bar Kokhba, who was proclaimed the Messiah by no less an authority than Rabbi Akiva. But this attempt did not fare any better, and was followed by a scorched earth policy meant to teach the Jews a lesson for all time.

The record of failure against Rome raised a question that Jews have faced in nearly every age: What is the proper response to misfortune—despair or hope? Early Rabbinic leaders were ambivalent in their answer. Given the horrors of exile and oppression under Roman rule, they were not in a position to squelch a belief that gave the people something to live for. At the same time, they could not be completely comfortable with a doctrine that had led to two disastrous wars and spawned a rival religion in the form of Christianity. As the historian Heinrich Graetz put it, messianism is both a Pandora's box and the elixir of life.[6]

Imagining the Messiah

Even if one accepts the idea of a messianic future, questions remain. What sort of person will the Messiah be—a Torah scholar who will inspire a return to God, or a warrior who will end foreign rule and reestablish Jewish sovereignty in Israel? When will the Messiah come—when things are so bad that only a superhuman figure can save the day, or when the Jewish people undergo a spiritual awakening on their own? Will the Messiah restore traditional practices such as animal sacrifice in a rebuilt

Temple, or introduce entirely new modes of worship? Will the Messiah work miracles or stay within the natural order?

Although Isaiah's promise of a righteous king who carries on the Davidic dynasty does not answer these questions, it makes it hard to avoid them. This is a clear case in which an ancient text puts us on a trajectory that goes far beyond what anyone in the ancient world could have imagined. To understand that trajectory and the full import of the text, we need to examine how subsequent generations tried to make sense of such an important doctrine.

FROM THE RABBIS TO MAIMONIDES

Faced with all these questions, the ancient Rabbis conceived a variety of responses. The most obvious one was to say that while belief in the coming of a Messiah is legitimate, it should not be foremost in one's mind. To them the foremost object in Judaism is—and always was—obedience to the commandments. This approach can be seen in the Mishnah (compiled around 200–250 CE), which included occasional references to a Messianic Age but nothing resembling a fully fleshed out theory.[7] Memories of the Bar Kokhba failure would have still been fresh in people's minds when it was compiled, and prudence likely dictated that the Rabbis not anger Roman authorities by stirring up messianic fervor yet again.

The crux of this alternative, as stated by the mishnaic scholar Jacob Neusner, is that the purpose of religious life is not salvation, understood as a future event, but sanctification, understood as an ever-present possibility.[8] God will send the Messiah at the appropriate time. If you want to please God, follow the commandments as articulated by the Rabbis. Beyond that, there is not much one can say. Along similar lines, the great talmudic sage Rav, who lived in the third century CE, maintained that the appointed dates for the Messiah have come and gone; so at this point, all that remains are repentance and good deeds (*Sanhedrin* 97b).

As the memory of Bar Kokhba receded and the center of Jewish learning moved from Israel to Babylonia, messianic speculation sprang up again. In the talmudic tractate *Sanhedrin*, there are any number of views about when the Messiah will come. One view has it that the Messiah will appear when the Jewish people repent for a single day or observe a single Sabbath in accordance with the Torah (*Sanhedrin* 97b).

In sharp contrast, another view holds that the Messiah will not arrive when life gets better, but when it gets markedly worse—when scholars are few in number, God-fearing men are despised, young men insult the old, daughters rise up against their mothers, and the whole kingdom succumbs to heresy (*Sanhedrin* 97a). The rationale for this view seems to be that if life becomes completely intolerable, God will have no choice but to intercede. In an attempt to honor both alternatives, Rabbi Yoḥanan concluded that the Messiah will come in a generation that is *either* totally righteous *or* totally corrupt (*Sanhedrin* 98a). Still another view maintains that before the Messiah comes, there will be cosmic upheavals involving sea monsters, a decisive battle between good and evil, or a complete deterioration in the quality of life (*Sanhedrin* 97a, *Sotah* 9:15). The dire nature of these predictions led some Rabbis to say that they did not want to live to see the Messiah because there would be so much suffering beforehand (*Sanhedrin* 98b).

Some Rabbis went so far as to say that the Messiah would usher in a time of abundance when women would give birth to children on the day of conception, trees would provide fruit on a daily basis, and cakes and wool garments would grow from the ground (*Shabbat* 30b). Against this, another tradition claimed that the only difference between this world and the days of the Messiah will be that, in the latter, Israel will regain political sovereignty (*Sanhedrin* 91b). Yet another tradition maintained there will be two Messiahs: the Messiah ben Joseph, who will win many victories but ultimately be slain, and the Messiah ben David, who will avenge the death of the first Messiah (possibly resurrecting him) and secure the ultimate victory over evil.[9] Finally, there is a tradition that imagined the Messiah as a leper at the gates of Rome, bandaging his sores (*Sanhedrin* 98a).

In short, there was no single Rabbinic position on the Messiah. As Neusner puts it: "The conception or category, Judaism's Messianic Doctrine, as a systematic construct, yields only confusion."[10] It was in an effort to clear up this confusion that Maimonides put forth a well-articulated theory of the Messiah in the last book of the *Mishnah Torah*.

The crux of Maimonides' position is that when the Messiah comes, there will be no cosmic upheaval or disruption of the natural order. The only difference between life now and life then will be that Israel will be at peace, regain political sovereignty, and be able to focus its attention on study and worship.[11] In regard to everything else, Maimonides wrote: "Do not think that the King Messiah will have to perform signs and wonders, bring anything new into being, revive the dead, or do similar things. It is not so."[12]

Maimonides had nothing but contempt for those who thought rivers would flow with wine, the earth would bring forth baked bread, or people would become angels. Even in the days of the Messiah, he believed, there would still be rich and poor, strong and weak.[13] People would still have to work to put food on their table. Yet, because wars would cease, it would be easier to procure the necessities of life. Maimonides also wrote that, in time, the Messiah would die a natural death just like any other person. It is clear, then, that Maimonides tried to demythologize our understanding of the Messiah. In simple terms, he depicted the days of the Messiah not as an earthly paradise where people will live like princes and princesses but as a time when study and worship will proceed without interruption. As he tells us: "The one preoccupation of the whole world will be to know the Lord."[14]

This did not mean that the Messiah will change things overnight. According to the philosopher Menachem Kellner, the Messianic Era is better understood as a process rather than an event.[15] We can see this in two ways. First, Maimonides tells us that the task of identifying the Messiah will proceed in stages: Rather than relying on astrological or numerical predictions, we will have to determine whether the person in question is a king from the House of David who meditates on the Torah, observes the commandments, prevails upon all of Israel to do so, and "fights the battles of the Lord." If all this comes to pass, Maimonides claims, we can *assume* that this person is the Messiah.[16] If he does all of this and rebuilds the Temple and gathers in the exiles, we can be sure he is. Not only will this take time; it will require active participation from a wide range of people who will have to cooperate with each other before the identity of the Messiah can be established. Second, Maimonides allows for the possibility that Christianity and Islam will play a role in educating people and, to use Kellner's expression, *monotheizing* the rest of humanity.[17] Again, this is to be done by natural means, which is to say that it will be accomplished by a gradual process of teaching and learning rather than a war or a sudden upheaval.

Maimonides' theory represents a major step forward if you believe, as I do, that progress is made when religious doctrines are subjected to rational critique. As he would say, the chief advantage of his theory is its appeal to the intellect rather than the imagination. Gone are the sort of images one sees in disaster movies or the lifestyles one associates with film stars. In their place are higher levels of knowledge and spiritual fulfillment.

In relinquishing the miraculous dimension of the Messianic Age, Maimonides creates another problem. If we retain the miraculous dimension, we raise the bar of acceptance for any pretender so high that it is nearly impossible to cross. If Elijah has not come to herald the Messiah's arrival, if the exiles have not returned to Zion, if rivers do not flow with wine, if no cataclysm or apocalypse has approached that described by the prophets, then the Messiah has not come, and we will have to go on waiting. Such a standard would have eliminated virtually all of the false messiahs mentioned above. If, however, we eliminate the miraculous dimension, we lower the bar of acceptance, and thus make it considerably easier—perhaps too easy?—for pretenders to make their case.

THE MESSIAH IN MODERNITY

As we have seen, the original conception of the Messiah was that of a king who will carry on the Davidic dynasty. As democratic movements took root, beginning with the American and French Revolutions, people began to question whether the Messiah had to be a king rather than just a charismatic leader. By the nineteenth century, belief in a personal Messiah began to wane, and for many people was replaced by belief in a

Messianic Age. According to the Jewish philosopher Hermann Cohen: "Therefore he can no longer have the meaning of an individual *person*; his dynastic designation, as in his general political and particularistic limitations, must be abandoned."[18] This is another way of saying that we should not expect an extraordinary person to appear on the scene, hold press conferences, or sign autographs. If Cohen is right, then questions like "Who is the Messiah?," "How will he make himself known?," or "How will we know that he is descended from David?" no longer have to be asked. Rather, we should think of messianism in moral terms: What must *we* do to correct injustice and bring about a more humane society?

Cohen also stresses the important difference between messianism as understood by the prophets and the idea of the Golden Age in Greek mythology. A return to the Golden Age takes us back to a state of lost innocence. But, Cohen insists, the prophets never speak of a return to the Garden of Eden before Adam and Eve ate the forbidden fruit. On the contrary, their idea is that humanity will go forward to a new and better age. According to Isaiah (11:9), it will not be an age of innocence, but an age when knowledge of God fills the earth as waters cover the sea.

For Cohen this means that the prophets introduced Western culture to the idea of the future.[19] It is not just that one day will follow another, but that the future will give us something different than anything we have known before. As we saw, Second Isaiah said that God is about to do something new. Again from Cohen: "The future is a postulate of religious faith and indeed its most wondrous flower."[20]

In addition to stressing the idea of a new and better future, Cohen also emphasizes the universal dimension of prophetic teaching. Hope, he writes, is transformed into faith when we no longer think of ourselves alone, which is to say when we associate the future with the emergence of a community whose concerns reach beyond family or friends — even national boundaries — and come to represent the community of humankind as a whole.[21] This, in Cohen's view, constitutes the crux of the messianic ideal. As he puts it: "The Messianic ideal offers man the consolation, confidence, and guarantee that not merely the chosen people but all nations will, at some future time, exist in harmony." In the words of Isaiah, knowledge of the Lord will not just cover Israel, but the entire earth.

Still, there is one aspect of Cohen's view that remains controversial: the idea of a Messiah who is always in the process of coming but never actually arrives. For Cohen, the Messianic Age represents an ideal of moral perfection, a condition in which all forms of injustice have been eliminated. He agrees with Kant that even though this ideal has never been achieved, we are obliged to work for its realization. Furthermore, he believes, the elimination of *all* forms of injustice will require not just an enormous effort, but an infinite effort. Morality, in his view, is a never-ending task. Though the future may be better than the past, it will never be everything morality demands. It follows that, no matter how much effort we expend, there will always be promises to keep, sins to confess, people to attend to, and institutions to safeguard.

This is Cohen's way of warning against complacency. He insists, however, that morality cannot amount to a labor of Sisyphus, where every time the hero rolls the rock up the hill, the gods see to it that it falls back down again.[22] Unlike Sisyphus, we can make ever closer approximations to moral perfection. As applied to the Messiah, this means that while the Messianic Age will never be realized in full, we can still hope that humanity will make progress toward it. Thus we can understand Cohen's claim: "His [the Messiah's] coming is not an actual end, but means merely the infinity of his coming, which in turn means the infinity of development."[23] In short, the Messianic Age is always ahead of us, always something to work for. As Steven Schwarzschild, a follower of Cohen, puts it: "The Messiah not only has not come but also will never have come . . . [rather] he will always be coming."[24]

Like Maimonides, Cohen eliminates the miraculous dimension of messianism. The natural order will remain as it is; only the moral order will change. By arguing for the Messiah's coming as an ideal rather than an actual end, he also closes any possibility of a pretender claiming he is the person everyone was waiting for. Yet, as one might expect, the idea of a Messiah who is always in the process of coming but never actually arrives does not appeal to everyone. After all, the whole point of messianism is to give people hope that the future will not repeat the mistakes of the past. If the Messiah (or the age he represents) never actually comes but is always in the process of coming, then, it would seem that, far from a guarantee of hope, belief in the Messiah is a guarantee of relative failure.[25]

To understand the difficulty Cohen gets into, suppose I asked you to walk to a location one hundred miles away. Although getting there would take time, it could be done. Ditto for a city one thousand miles away. But now suppose I asked you to walk to a location that is infinitely far away. The problem is not that infinity is a large or even a very large number. Rather, given the nature of infinity, no matter how many steps you take, you will still have an infinite number of steps to go. Applying this reasoning to the Messiah, the conclusion is clear: The Messiah will only come at eternity. As Franz Rosenzweig objected, what only comes *at* eternity does not come *for all* eternity.[26] If the Messiah is not coming for all eternity, then he is not coming at all. How, then, can belief in the Messiah offer hope?

My response is to say that Cohen is half right. He is right to eradicate miracles, kingship, and anything that might contribute to a personality cult. He is also right to say that history cannot determine the standards of morality. Just because no society to date has eliminated all forms of corruption, it does not follow that we should give up trying. Again, per Levinas, the distinguishing feature of Jewish existence is its ability to stand apart from history and be its judge.

Where I think Cohen goes wrong is his claim that morality presents us with an infinite task, and therefore the ideal of a Messianic Age can never be fully realized. Though Judaism does ask us to strive for goals that exceed the capabilities of any one person, I do not believe that it asks us to strive for goals that are infinitely far off. My position is an outgrowth of Deuteronomy 30:11–14:

Surely, this Instruction which I enjoin upon you this day is not too baffling for you, nor is it beyond reach. It is not in the heavens, that you should say, "Who among us can go up to the heavens and get it for us and impart it to us, that we may observe it?" Neither is it beyond the sea, that you should say, "Who among us can cross to the other side of the sea and get it for us and impart it to us, that we may observe it?" No, the thing is very close to you, in your mouth and in your heart, to observe it.

I take this to mean that God does not ask us to do anything we are incapable of doing. If God wants us to end war and treat the poor with respect, then we must have it within our power to do so.

In essence, I believe that a Messianic Age can be attained, and that if there has been any delay in realizing it, the fault lies with us. From my perspective, then, the sharp rebukes that occupy so much of prophetic literature are perfectly justified so long as present reality falls short of divine commands. With these points in mind, I am partial to a Rabbinic legend that says the Messiah will come when all Israel observes the Sabbath two weeks running. On the one hand, we have realism: No one thinks this is likely to happen any time soon. On the other hand, we have a requisite degree of optimism: Nothing stands in the way of realizing it except a concerted effort on our part. In principle, the Messianic Age is never more than thirteen days off.

Hope and Moral Progress

Our discussion has taken us a long way from the pages of Isaiah. But that in itself is astonishing, because it means that after more than 2,500 years, Isaiah has become a significant part of Jewish self-understanding, and continues to inspire us. Although some of the details accompanying the prophet's vision have since been modified, including the idea that the Messiah will rule as a king, its central theme remains intact. The way things are is not the way they have to be — or, in time, the way they will be, if we do what the prophets teach us. If we are going to be true to the prophetic view of religion, it is not enough, for example, to offer lip service by reciting the standard prayers for the Messiah to come. Prayer is only meaningful if it is a spur to action. As long as the poor are neglected, the courts permit special treatment for the rich and powerful, and merchants cheat their customers, which is to say as long as history repeats itself, the Messiah—or the age that bears his name—will not arrive.

Although the promise of a better future has held special significance for generations of Jews who have suffered oppression, its appeal is universal. Without hope, there is despair. Despair, in turn, is the enemy of moral progress. As the Christian theologian Jurgen Moltmann remarked, it is no accident that above the entrance to Dante's hell is the inscription "Abandon hope, all ye who enter."[27] So while the Messiah has still not come—at least as Jews see it—the promise of his coming speaks to an elemental feature of the human psyche: the need to face the future with confidence.

CHAPTER 5

Jeremiah

Suffering for the Sake of God

My heart is crushed within me,
All my bones are trembling;
I have become like a drunken man,
Like one overcome by wine
Because of the LORD and His holy word.

—JEREMIAH 23:9

It should be clear by now that being a prophet is no fun. In most cases, one has to carry an unpopular message to the people and face the usual scorn and humiliation that goes with it. Nobody wants to hear that unless drastic changes are made in the social order and the religious commitment of the people, God will execute judgment on the kingdom. On top of that, in the ancient and medieval worlds, as in much of the modern world, free speech was not guaranteed. Accusing priests and official prophets of misconduct would create powerful enemies, while predicting the defeat or downfall of the king could be viewed as treason.

Of all the prophets, Jeremiah is the most explicit about the difficulty of carrying an unpopular message to a hostile audience. He tells us in the opening verses that during his ministry—which began in the days of King Josiah (around 627 BCE) and continued for more than forty years through the reigns of Jehoiakim and Zedekiah—the people of his hometown of Anathoth plotted against him (11:21–23). A priest named

Pashhur had him beaten and put in the stocks, with his ankles and wrists locked up overnight (20:1–3). When Jeremiah opposes a Judean alliance with Egypt and urges surrender to the Babylonians instead, he is sent to prison (37:21). Eventually a group of priests and official prophets charge that his message of surrender is sowing discontent among the soldiers and, with Zedekiah's approval, lower him into a cistern, where he goes without water and almost dies.

Fortunately, Zedekiah undergoes a change of heart and sends people to rescue him (38:1–28). After his release, Zedekiah has a private conversation with Jeremiah and warns him not to reveal its contents. Although Jeremiah never discloses the exchange, he is nonetheless sent back to prison, where he remained until Jerusalem fell to the Babylonians in 586 BCE. Following the destruction of Jerusalem, Jeremiah went into exile in Egypt. We do not know the circumstances of his death.

The people's animosity toward Jeremiah is especially strong because he goes much farther than the prophets before him. Whereas Isaiah said that God would never abandon Jerusalem, the site of the Holy Temple, Jeremiah insists that the Temple will fall if the people continue their evil ways. In one place, he reports God as saying: "Shall I not bring retribution / On a nation such as this?" (5:9). He even warns the people not to take refuge in the Temple when the day of retribution arrives (7:4).

Still, it would be wrong to think of Jeremiah as all doom and gloom, because he does offer words of consolation. For example, at 24:4–7, he promises that those who return from the exile will find favor if they turn back to God with all their heart. As we saw, he also envisions a time when God will make a new covenant with Israel and remember the people's sins no more.[1] But, of course, the new covenant is in the future — a hallmark of the Messianic Age, when Israel will finally come to its senses.

Meanwhile, the day-to-day situation Jeremiah witnessed was bleak. Jehoiakim used forced labor to build a luxurious palace at a time when fraud and violence ruled the day. The familiar pleas to care for the widow and the orphan were ignored. Murder and theft went on unchecked. Offerings were made to strange gods. Although he was mocked every place he went, Jeremiah tells us that he cannot keep silent. God's words burn in him like a fire so that he cannot hold them in (20:9).

The details of Jeremiah's life raise important questions. How could an all-powerful God, a God who parted the Red Sea and destroyed the mightiest army on earth, allow the Temple, the seat of divine authority, to be destroyed by a pagan nation, in this case a nation that worships Marduk? Or, on a more personal level: How could an all-powerful God allow a chosen servant to be treated in such a disrespectful manner? I will address both of these questions, the second one before the first. But before I do, I want to turn back and examine the prophet par excellence — Moses, who also led a difficult and tumultuous life.

The Reluctant Prophet Who Led the Israelites out of Egypt

When God first calls to Moses at Exodus 3, the Israelites are enslaved to a brutal dictator who has ordered all Israelite male children to be thrown into the Nile. Under the circumstances, we would expect Moses to be eager to serve God and liberate his people. But the ensuing dialogue shows that Moses is anything but. Time and again he raises objections to God's plan for action: "Who am I that I should go before Pharaoh?" "Who shall I say has sent me?" "What if the Israelites will not listen to me?" "I am slow of speech." By Exodus 3:13, he pleads with God to choose someone else. Tired of hearing excuses, God becomes angry with Moses.

Why is Moses so reluctant?[2] One way to answer this question is to recall a passage from Plato's *Republic*, where the characters agree that the best people to rule a state are those who are least eager to do so.[3] After viewing civil disorder for much of his life, Plato thought that those who are eager to rule often put their own interests above those of the state. In other words, they want to rule so they can cash in on the benefits that come with high office. By contrast, those who are not eager to rule are more likely to put the interests of the state first, because they have no desire for wealth or power. In a biblical context, we can broaden this insight to say that a reluctant leader would not be inclined to put her own interests ahead of God's for the simple reason that, aside from God's exhortation, she would never accept the job. Measured by this standard, Moses is the ultimate servant. Rather than bask in the limelight of being the one to lead the Israelites out of Egypt, he is cautious. At Numbers 12:3, the Torah calls attention to his humility. In the end, his decision to assume the mantle of leadership rests on his readiness to carry out the will of God and nothing else.

As we have seen, carrying out the will of God is not for the faint of heart. No sooner do the people celebrate their release from slavery than they begin to complain of hunger, thirst, and the hardships of the desert. Although God provides them with manna, that is not enough. They want the lavish meals they think they enjoyed in Egypt (Num. 11:4–5). Later, at Numbers 14, they beg to be taken back to Egypt, indicating that, despite all Moses has done for them, they prefer to be slaves to Pharaoh. In addition to disloyalty, Moses must deal with the apostasy of the Golden Calf, challenges to his authority from Aaron and Miriam, and the outbreak of civil war.

Nor is that all. As difficult as it is to please the people, it sometimes proves just as difficult to please God. Twice (Exod. 32 and Num. 14) God becomes angry with the people and threatens to destroy them. Each time Moses must placate God and ask God to reconsider the decision. Heschel is therefore right to say that the prophet often finds himself in a lonely position: When he is with the people, he pleads for God; when he is with God, he pleads for the people.[4] In this way, the prophet occupies a no-man's-land between heaven and earth. Wherever things go wrong, he is the one who has to set them right.

We know that at the end of his life, Moses is not allowed to enter the Promised Land. It would be one thing if God were to console him by revealing a vision of the next generation of Israelites living happily in the land and taking full advantage of the milk and honey it has to offer. Though Moses himself could not participate, he could die a happy man, knowing that his labors in the desert had not been in vain. Instead, at Deuteronomy 31, God predicts that the next generation will repeat all of its parents' mistakes. For all of Moses' efforts, then, God and the people will remain at odds with one another.

With the possible exception of the "Song at the Sea" at Exodus 15, when the Israelites are rescued from Pharaoh's army, it is hard to find a point in the story of the Exodus when Moses experiences anything in the way of happiness. And even that moment is short-lived; the people begin to complain a few lines later. Rather than happiness, what appears to keep Moses going is an unshakeable sense of duty to carry out God's will no matter what the obstacles. As we have seen, his understanding of that duty drives him to even call God to account.

The Reluctant Prophet Who Witnessed the Fall of Jerusalem

In many ways, Moses sets the tone for Jeremiah. Although there is no burning bush in Jeremiah's call, as Buber says, it descends into the human situation unexpected and unwilled, free and fresh like lightning.[5]

> Before I created you in the womb, I selected you;
> Before you were born, I consecrated you;
> I appointed you a prophet concerning the nations. (1:5)

Rather than accept the call without thinking, Jeremiah protests that he is too young and not a good enough speaker to take on such a role.

Again, God is not swayed by excuses. Jeremiah is the one to carry God's word, and that is that:

> So you, gird up your loins,
> Arise and speak to them
> All that I command you.
> Do not break down before them,
> Lest I break you before them.
> I make you this day
> A fortified city,
> And an iron pillar,
> And bronze walls
> Against the whole land—
> Against Judah's kings and officers,

And against its priests and citizens.
They will attack you,
But they shall not overcome you;
For I am with you—declares the LORD—to save you. (1:17–19)

The rhetoric of this passage suggests that Jeremiah is about to go to war with the powers that be, both secular and religious. Like Moses, he will occupy the no-man's-land between heaven and earth, pleading for mercy with one and for a moral awakening with the other. In the words of Buber, he is the messenger of God *and* intercessor in one.[6]

Also like Moses, he is not afraid to hold God to account. At 12:1, he raises the classic formulation of the problem of evil:

You will win, O LORD, if I make claim against You,
Yet I shall present charges against You:
Why does the way of the wicked prosper?

And yet, for all his honesty in the face of God, Jeremiah responds with an unshakeable sense of duty:

You enticed me, O LORD, and I was enticed;
You overpowered me and You prevailed.
I have become a constant laughingstock,
Everyone jeers at me. . . .
But [God's word] was like a raging fire in my heart,
Shut up in my bones;
I could not hold it in, I was helpless. (20:7–9)

The emotional intensity of this passage is impossible to miss. The difference between Jeremiah and Moses is that while Moses is silent about his inner turmoil, Jeremiah is explicit about his.

To understand this turmoil, we must not forget that while Jeremiah is disgusted by what he sees the people doing, they are nonetheless *his* people—and, just as important, *God's* people too. In anguish, he reports God as saying:

> I have abandoned My House,
> I have deserted My possession,
> I have given over My dearly beloved
> Into the hands of her enemies. (12:7)

As the servant of God, Jeremiah feels the same anguish over the fate of his countrymen:

> Oh, my suffering, my suffering!
> How I writhe!
> Oh, the walls of my heart! (4:19)

The Hebrew is more explicit, for it has Jeremiah saying that he can feel the anguish deep in his bowels.

The same sentiment is expressed when disaster strikes:

> My heart is sick within me. . . .
> Because my people is shattered I am shattered;
> I am dejected, seized by desolation.
> Is there no balm in Gilead?
> Can no physician be found?
> Why has healing not yet
> Come to my poor people?
> Oh, that my head were water,
> My eyes a fount of tears!
> Then would I weep day and night
> For the slain of my poor people. (8:18–23)

So troubling is Jeremiah's predicament that at 20:14, he curses the day of his birth and asks why he has had to see so much misery and spend his days in shame.

The simple answer is that he lived through the fall of Jerusalem and, like Cassandra of Greek mythology, was ignored by those he sought to warn. As he tells us, the people have eyes but do not see, ears but do not hear (5:21). Why is this? Christian commentators see in Jeremiah evidence of the sickness of the human heart and thus the doctrine of original sin, which holds that depravity is inherent in the human condition.[7] At 5:23 and again at 17:9, Jeremiah says that the human heart is stubborn and rebellious, weak and deceitful. It is no accident that Kant, a Pietist Christian, argued more than two thousand years later that human behavior is affected by a perversity of the heart that runs so deep, it cannot be eradicated.[8] He meant that even when we think we are acting in a moral fashion, an element of selfishness is always corrupting our motivation. But Jeremiah himself never asserted anything that radical. The human heart may be stubborn and rebellious at times, but to him it was not sinful at its core because there is always hope that one day human beings will renounce sin and return to God.

Understanding Jeremiah's Suffering

Let us return to the question of why God would allow a chosen servant to suffer such humiliation. In time, another prophet, Second Isaiah, suggests an answer: Contrary to what we might think, it is the one who suffers most, who is shunned and despised, who is the true servant of God.

> Who can believe what we have heard?
> Upon whom has the arm of the LORD been revealed?
> For he has grown, by His favor, like a tree crown,
> Like a tree trunk out of arid ground.
> He had no form or beauty, that we should look at him:
> No charm, that we should find him pleasing.
> He was despised, shunned by men,
> A man of suffering, familiar with disease.
> As one who hid his face from us,
> He was despised, we held him of no account. (Isa. 53:1–3)

The meaning of the passage has long been disputed: Jews see it as a reference to Israel's place among the nations, while Christians see it as foretelling the coming of Jesus.⁹ In either case, we must ask why suffering should confer legitimacy.

We can begin to answer this by considering the opposite: someone who has never suffered in any appreciable way. Imagine someone on whom fortune seems to have smiled from the moment of her birth. Her family loved her. She has always been popular. She received a quality education and went on to a wonderful job. She has an adoring husband and equally adoring children. She has never experienced rejection either in her personal or business life. As a result, she has always maintained a confident and cheerful disposition. Recognizing this, her colleagues and community have honored her with a variety of awards.

Although it is tempting to think that God must look favorably on such a person, the relevant question is, would she would be a legitimate spokesperson for God, especially during a time of crisis? Has someone who has never dealt with misfortune earned the right to speak about the meaning of life? For my part, the answer is no. Human beings are inherently vulnerable. A person who has never dealt with a broken heart, never had to endure intense pain, or never walked the streets wondering how she would support her family has not experienced enough of life to be able to talk about it with any degree of understanding. Moreover, a person who has never had to deal with misfortune has never had to call on the moral strength needed to overcome it. As is discussed in chapter 8, this is the point Satan makes at the beginning of Job. How can we trust the moral fiber of someone whose life has been a cakewalk?

The obvious answer is that we cannot. Qualities like faith, courage, love, or commitment to an ideal have to be tested to be real. Abraham was tested, repeatedly. So was Moses. It is for this reason that suffering can be ennobling, that we can admire those who are beset with pain, written off, or cast aside, but remain true to their calling. As committed an atheist as Bertrand Russell saw in the endurance of intense pain "a sacredness and an overpowering awe."¹⁰

We should keep in mind, however, that some of those who suffer feel the agony of others' misfortunes. Concerned parents may suffer at the sight of their child in pain. Morally sensitive people may be dismayed by the sight of a homeless person on a bitterly cold day. Along these lines, Kant argued that we should not avoid places like hospitals or debtors' prisons where the poor suffer, because we have a moral duty to cultivate the compassionate side of our nature.[11]

On this point, Cohen goes further than Kant, arguing that for the prophets, the fundamental problem of human life is not death but poverty. For Cohen, poverty is the chief way human vulnerability expresses itself — or, as he put it, the poor person typifies humanity in general.[12] Broadly speaking, the main purpose of the prophets' teaching is to highlight the importance of compassion. Compassion, Cohen says, more than anything else, enables us to establish a bond with our fellow human beings. It is when I take pity on another person that the person becomes more than just another face in the crowd but a friend or fellow (German, *mitmensch*), by which he means a person whose welfare is tied up with my own.[13] To this Cohen would add that if, as the prophets insist, there is a divine command to help those at the bottom of the social scale, then by establishing a bond of fellowship with them, I become a worthy human being in my own right.[14] In the immortal words of Hillel: If I am only for myself, what am I?

It is here above all else that Jeremiah excels. It is not just his own misfortune he is bemoaning but, more importantly, the plight of the widows, orphans, and oppressed laborers whose cause he has taken up. Their suffering is his suffering. In Buber's words: "His 'I' is so deeply set in the 'I' of the people that his life cannot be regarded as that of an individual."[15] Moreover, this type of suffering — not only with but on behalf of other people — is tinged with outrage, and therefore provides a springboard for corrective action. So even though Jeremiah's writings reveal a tortured soul overcome by the sight of poverty and injustice, we can also see them as ennobling. As troubled as he is, we can admire Jeremiah as a human being considerably more than we can a person who goes through life without a care in the world.

There is another reason why God allows Jeremiah to undergo such turmoil—and it has to do with the fact that God undergoes turmoil as well. The book of Deuteronomy tells us that God chose Israel out of love (3:7, 7:8) and wants to be loved in return (6:5). But as we have seen throughout this study, God is spurned at nearly every turn. Divine commandments are broken. The witnesses to God's great name are ostracized. Worship falls into the hands of false prophets and hypocritical priests. God's hope that Israel will become a light unto the other nations now seems futile. In this light, perhaps it is not surprising that God allows a chosen servant to be humiliated—because when the people turn their backs on God, there is a sense in which God is humiliated as well. If Jeremiah is outraged by what he sees, so is God. If Jeremiah is torn between his feelings for his people and his disgust at what they have become, God is as well.

It could be said, therefore, that Jeremiah's turmoil is symbolic of God's turmoil. If so, he would not have been the first prophet to serve God in this way. Recall how Hosea's torment over an unfaithful wife was symbolic of God's torment over an unfaithful Israel. In either case, a servant who lived a comfortable and successful life during a period of moral and spiritual crisis would have been totally out of place.

As for why an all-powerful God would allow the Temple to be destroyed, the prophetic answer is that, despite repeated warnings about provoking God, the people are no longer worthy of it. By the same token, if Israel were loyal to God, then there is no way that a pagan nation could defeat it. But, in Jeremiah's opinion, this has not happened. We must be careful, then, not to view this—or any other conflict—as a victory for Israel's opponent. It is not that God has decided that the Babylonians are now the chosen people. Rather, it is that Israel has failed God and deserves what it gets.

I will take up this issue again when I discuss Ezekiel. At this point, it is noteworthy that Persia conquered Babylonia, and Cyrus of Persia allowed the Jews to return to Jerusalem and rebuild what the Babylonians had destroyed. But, as indicated earlier, the Romans destroyed the rebuilt Temple in 70 CE. Although both cases of destruction are seen as national tragedies, Hosea may have spoken for all the prophets when he said, more than 150 years before the Babylonian invasion: "I desire mercy, not sacrifice, / the knowledge of God rather than burnt offerings."[16]

Prophecy and Social Status

Putting all this together, we arrive at the conclusion that people like Moses or Jeremiah do not live their lives the way most of us do. For most of us, the pursuit of happiness is the predominant factor in decision making. What college will provide the best opportunity to land a good job? What job will provide the best opportunity for advancement? When is the best time to have children, if one is going to have them at all?

As prevalent as it is, this way of thinking is exactly what the prophets reject. For them, there is only one path to take: carry the word of God to the people no matter the consequences. Even though God tells Jeremiah, "You shall say all these things to them, but they will not listen to you; you shall call to them, but they will not respond to you" (7:27), Jeremiah still chooses the life of a dissident. Once God's words come to him like a raging fire in his heart, he is incapable of doing otherwise.

This does not mean that all dissidents are prophets—far from it. Rather, it means that people like Jeremiah who feel a burning desire to serve God are not motivated by the things that most of us hold dear. Wealth, popularity, and social position mean nothing to them. If anything, they are suspicious of them. They are willing to suffer any amount of external (as well as internal) abuse if that is what it takes to serve God. Put otherwise, service to God is self-justifying: to be called by God is reason enough to act. Once the call comes, nothing else matters.

Nevertheless, we must steer clear of hasty generalizations. Although Jeremiah went to war with the powers that be, not all biblical prophets did. Moses had a difficult time leading an unruly people through the desert, but there was never any serious question that he was in charge. Those who challenged his authority, including Aaron and Miriam, paid a price. David was victorious in battle and reigned as king. Solomon reigned as king and amassed legendary wealth. Although these people faced obstacles and sometimes came up short, it would be hard to describe them as dissidents.

If there is a lesson to be learned, it is that the circumstances of people's lives are not always a reliable guide to whether their claim to speak for God is authentic. Some prophets occupy the top of the social ladder, some the bottom. Some lead schools, while others act alone. Some come from priestly families, while others are of common birth. From what we can tell, God selects messengers from a variety of backgrounds. This means we have no choice but to look beyond their social status to the content of their message. Someone who turns a blind eye to injustice, who takes a casual attitude to idolatry, or who modifies his principles to placate existing centers of power cannot speak for God.

The problem is that while these criteria allow us to tell who does *not* speak for God, they do not necessarily allow us to tell who does. In the Torah, a pillar of cloud descended on the Tent of Meeting when Moses and God communicated, leaving no doubt as to the legitimacy of Moses' prophecy. But nothing like this validated the prophets who make up the subject matter of this book. In their case, the people were faced with a choice and, in most cases, chose incorrectly. The people were willing to live with bribes, false weights and measures, and letting widows and orphans fend for themselves. They sought mechanical ways to curry favor with fortune, such as turning to idols or sacrificing animals. When someone stood up to say all of this is wrong, they spurned both the message and the messenger.

While we may never have a simple formula for identifying true prophets, the history of prophecy leaves us with the question of whether we have become so set in our ways, so comfortable with the powers that be, that we too have turned our backs on people who speak the truth—and thus on God as well.

CHAPTER 6

Ezekiel

Freedom and Responsibility

> Cast away all the transgressions by which you
> offended, and get yourselves a new heart
> and a new spirit.
>
> —EZEKIEL 18:31

No matter how you approach him, Ezekiel is a controversial figure. A younger contemporary of Jeremiah, he was exiled to Babylonia in 597 BCE. His prophecy is estimated to have extended from 593 to 571 BCE, and therefore included the fall of Jerusalem. The Rabbis wondered why his writings ever came to be included in the biblical cannon and forbade public discussion of his most famous vision.[1] Abraham Joshua Heschel's two-volume study of the prophets excludes him. Yet, despite all of this, Cohen treats Ezekiel as the supreme prophet. Let us therefore look at the varied reactions to his legacy.

A Legitimate Prophet?

The first reason for the negative reactions to Ezekiel has to do with location. Unlike the visions of the other prophets, Ezekiel's came to him outside the Land of Israel, when he was living in Babylonia. To be sure, God had spoken to Abraham and Moses when they were outside Israel, but that was before Israel became a state of its own. Once such a state was founded and once worship became centralized in Jerusalem, a number of Jewish thinkers became skeptical of revelations that occurred anywhere else. Along these lines, Psalm 137:4 asks: "How can we sing a song of the LORD on alien soil?"[2] The mishnaic treatise *Kelim* (1:6–8) says that the Land of Israel is holier than all other lands, that Jerusalem is the holiest city, and that the Temple Mount is the holiest place in Jerusalem.[3] Along similar lines, the medieval philosopher Judah Halevi argued that the Land of Israel is the center of the earth and that prophecy can exist only in it or with reference to it.[4]

Despite the importance of Jerusalem, Ezekiel claims to see the glory of the Lord *depart* from it (10–11) because the people are no longer worthy of God. In his words (8:10), it now contains "all detestable forms of creeping things and beasts and all the fetishes of the House of Israel." Under these circumstances, God has no choice but to reach out to someone living in exile and warn that Jerusalem is about to fall. Even if we discount this vision, we would do well to question the suggestion that Jerusalem or anywhere else is the center of the world. The God who called the prophets to service is, after all, the God who created all of heaven and earth and whose rule extends from the netherworld to the high heavens. Buber is therefore right to say that from our vantage point, the notion that there is a center of the world amounts to false pride and confidence.[5]

Beyond the question of location, Ezekiel's relation to Israel and Jerusalem is still problematic. One does not have to read very far through Jeremiah to see that God is not pleased with Jerusalem and is ready to hold it accountable for its sins. Nonetheless, Jeremiah holds out hope that if the people give up their evil ways and return to God, God will forget the punishment in store for them.[6] Granted, the prospect of a whole culture changing its ways is remote, but whereas Jeremiah did his best to bring it about, with Ezekiel, the time for repentance has passed: Jerusalem, which he refers to as a "bloody city," has become so detestable in God's eyes that its destruction is certain.[7]

The ferocity of Ezekiel's condemnation of Jerusalem goes well beyond anything articulated by his predecessors. The God described as abounding in mercy and graciousness at Exodus 34, the God who in Jeremiah

(12:7–9) lamented the destruction of Jerusalem, will now have no pity on it.[8] On the contrary, God will destroy it and mock it among the other nations of the world. The people living there will be so desperate, they will resort to cannibalism. What hope there is for restoration will rest with the exiles. Even when restoration does occur, it will not be because the people have returned to God, but because God wants to preserve the sanctity of the divine name (Ezek. 36:22–23). In other words, restoration will not be for Israel's sake, but for God's alone.[9]

Worse, perhaps, the sexual detail that Ezekiel uses to characterize Israel's sinful ways has no precedent in the earlier prophets. Though both Hosea and Jeremiah compare Israel to a wayward spouse or prostitute, Ezekiel's use of this metaphor in chapters 16 and 23 is so explicit that even in our age, when sex and violence suffuse movies and television shows, it is hard to read them without cringing.[10]

Yet another outlier is the fertility of Ezekiel's imagination. Although all the prophets had lively imaginations, Ezekiel's far exceeds anyone else's. In several places, including the famous Dry Bones vision of chapter 37, he reports out-of-body experiences in which he is transported to different locations.[11] In other places, God tells him to eat a scroll (3:1–3), eat bread baked over cow dung (4:15), and cut his hair with a sword (5:1). He is also told not to mourn the death of his wife (24:15–17). While it is not hard to find symbolic significance in these acts, many indicate depression or desperation. All raise the tricky question of where to draw the line between fantasy and reality.

Ezekiel's most famous vision occurs in chapter 1, when he sees a storm cloud with flashing fire approaching from the North. In the center of the cloud, he sees the appearance of the glory (*kavod*) of God "in human form" sitting on a throne carried by a four-wheeled chariot. On each side of the chariot are mythological creatures (cherubim) with four faces — those of a human, a lion, an ox, and an eagle — and four wings. Below the wings are human hands. A radiant fire keeps moving among them. Finally, the wheels of the chariot are covered with eyes.

How are we to understand this? Today, we read it on Shavuot to commemorate the revelation at Sinai because both describe a dramatic theophany or appearance of God to humans. It should be noted, however, that the Rabbis forbade anyone from discussing the chariot vision in public (*Ḥagigah* 13 a–b) on the grounds that it was so esoteric it could lead one astray if one did not have sufficient training to deal with it. In time, it became a foundational text for Jewish mysticism, as generations of like-minded people described similar ascents into heaven.[12]

Maimonides, who thought that all prophets were first and foremost philosophers, identified Ezekiel's vision with what the Greeks called divine science or metaphysics. He therefore took the chariot vision (*ma'aseh merkavah*) to be an account of the heavenly realm.[13] According to this interpretation, the wheels of the chariot represent the spheres whose rotation carries the stars and planets in their transit around the earth.[14] Yet Maimonides' reading of the passage is itself obscure and difficult to interpret—in part because he did not want to violate the Rabbinic prohibition against discussing it in public. Alternatively, he may have thought the science behind it was flawed: There would have to be more than four heavenly spheres to account for the observed phenomena.[15]

The result is that after 2,500 years of speculation, no one can say for sure what the chariot vision means. Much the same is true of chapters 38–39, which describe an apocalyptic battle involving Gog from the land of Magog. In Jewish tradition, this came to stand for the final battle of good against evil that would herald the coming of the Messiah, and in Christian tradition, the final battle of Satan against Jesus. Later traditions take it to refer to Napoleon's invasion of Europe or the collapse of the Soviet Union.

The final reason for the negative reaction, and from a Rabbinic point of view the most important, is Ezekiel's vision of a restored Temple in chapters 42–48. Not only were his architectural plans not followed, but his description of holidays and sacrifices does not cohere with laws set forth in the Torah. For example, his account of the holidays in chapter 45 omits Shavuot and seems to replace Yom Kippur with something else. In the same chapter, he introduces sacrifices that are not mentioned in the Torah and, in one instance (45:23), conflict with the procedure set forth at Numbers 28:19. Furthermore, in the preceding chapter (44) he demotes the Levitical priests on the grounds that they are being punished for idolatrous practices.

Not surprisingly, the Rabbis struggled to make sense of these discrepancies. Was his account of the sacrifices supposed to describe inaugural ceremonies, when departures were made from standard procedures? Was he talking about a Messianic Era, when, according to some accounts, the laws of the Torah would be modified? Worst of all, did he knowingly introduce innovations in religious law, putting his prophecy on a par with that of Moses? Or, was he not familiar with all the details of the Torah?

Although no one knows what Ezekiel was thinking, that should not stop us from looking more closely at his legacy. How, for example, did such a controversial figure become so important to Cohen that he ascribed to Ezekiel a new understanding of what it means to be human—and with it, a new understanding of God as well?[16]

Only the Sinner Shall Die

From a philosophic perspective, Ezekiel is best known for his view on individual responsibility. As readers of the Torah soon learn, moral responsibility is often corporate in the sense that God often looks at a family, a city, or even a whole nation as a single agent, to be rewarded or punished collectively. When setting forth the Second Commandment at Exodus 20:5, God says: "For I the LORD God am an impassioned God, visiting the guilt of the parents upon the children, upon the third and upon the fourth generations of those who reject Me, but showing kindness to the thousandth generation of those who love Me and keep My commandments."

Similar language occurs at Exodus 34:7, where God promises to visit the iniquity of parents upon children and children's children, down to the third and fourth generations. In addition to these passages, God slays the firstborn of the Egyptians in order to punish Pharaoh (Exod. 12:29), commands the killing of Amalekite children (Deut. 25:17–19), and allows Satan to kill Job's children as a test of his faith (Job 1:18–

19).[17] Leviticus and Deuteronomy contain elaborate rewards and curses that will be visited on the whole nation depending on how it behaves.[18]

The Torah is hardly the only place where moral responsibility extends across generations. In Greek mythology, the sin of Tantalus is so grievous that, in addition to his punishment, a curse is put on his descendants until the time of Orestes, when it takes a jury trial and a threat from Athena to remove it. Even today, innocent people may suffer when an unscrupulous ruler puts a whole nation in peril to further his own interests.

Against this way of looking at things, Ezekiel protests: "The word of the LORD came to me: What do you mean by quoting this proverb upon the soil of Israel, 'Parents eat sour grapes and the children's teeth are blunted [or set on edge]'? As I live—declares the LORD God—this proverb shall no longer be current among you in Israel. Consider, all lives are Mine; the life of the parent and the life of the child are both Mine. The person who sins, only he shall die" (18:1–4). The proverb about eating sour grapes must have been well-known, because Jeremiah cites it as well (31:29). Its doctrine is essentially that as found in the Torah: If the parents sin, the children will inherit their guilt.

Ezekiel then says that the Torah's conception of responsibility cannot be right: "A child shall not share the burden of a parent's guilt, nor shall a parent share the burden of a child's guilt; the righteousness of the righteous shall be accounted to him alone, and the wickedness of the wicked shall be accounted to him alone" (18:20). Even a person's past actions do not determine his moral standing in the present: "If a wicked one repents of all the sins that he committed and keeps all My laws and does what is just and right, he shall live; he shall not die" (18:21). On the other hand: "If a righteous person turns away from his righteousness and does wrong, practicing the very abominations that the wicked person practiced . . . he shall die" (18:24).

Although the doctrine of individual responsibility is stated with remarkable clarity, we cannot be certain that Ezekiel himself would have accepted all its implications. At 9:5 he indicates that God will show no pity in destroying Jerusalem, killing young and old, women and children alike.[19] At 21:8 he claims that God will wipe out both the righteous and the wicked. Throughout his writings, he longs for the restoration of the sacrificial cult, where the priests are charged with atoning for the sins of the entire nation.

The lack of consistency should not surprise us. It is not unusual for prophetic utterances collected over a period of twenty or more years to contain conflicting opinions. Moreover, Ezekiel is hardly the only thinker who failed to appreciate the full implications of his own ideas. In a later age, Maimonides argued that the body is a hindrance to the acquisition of knowledge.[20] But he also held that reincarnation, when the soul is put back into a body, is an essential part of Jewish belief.[21] Even granting Ezekiel's lack of consistency, there is no denying that he has hit on an important point: Unlike property or genetic traits, sin cannot be transferred from one generation to the next. Because we alone are responsible for our sins, we cannot be held accountable for what our parents did — or, for that matter, what Adam and Eve did.

What is more, if sin is not transferable, neither is atonement. In view of this, we must reject the idea that someone else could die for our sins. In the words of Kant: "The human being must make or have made *himself* into whatever he is or should become in a moral sense, good or evil."[22] It is this insight that led Cohen to say that Ezekiel introduced a new understanding of what it means to be human. While the other prophets stressed the social nature of sin, Ezekiel is the first one to focus on the individual, asking: How do *I* deal with the sins I have committed? This focus is evident in his statement (at 18:20): "The person who sins, he alone shall die." He means that we alone bear responsibility for our actions — not God, not our ancestors, not the alignment of the stars, not an evil impulse implanted in us at our birth.[23] When it comes to the moral worth of our actions, we should look no further than ourselves.

To take Ezekiel's insight one step further, we must look to ourselves even when discussing larger problems that afflict society. If Amos's criticisms are still valid, if, for example, neglect of the poor is a feature of modern society, then I must ask myself: What have *I* done to contribute to it, and what can *I* do to help eliminate it? If all I focus on are abstract social forces, such as the seemingly intractable nature of poverty, then I am passing the buck. In Cohen's words: "Call every single man who participates in the affairs of the state, or in the press, or in the other countless administrative organs, call him as an individual before the tribunal of his conscience."[24]

Assume for the moment that Cohen is right. Suppose I tell a lie and take full responsibility for what I have done. Suppose that my conscience is developed enough that I feel guilty. What should I do to deal with my guilt? Here, Cohen thinks that religion goes beyond ethics. Ethics tells me that lying is wrong, but, under the circumstances, that is not very helpful. Once the act is done, it becomes an unalterable fact. Besides, I already know that lying is wrong and feel awful for having done it. The question is how I can reconcile with myself by relieving the guilt that lowers me in my own eyes. Without some way to cope with guilt, my feelings of inadequacy might accumulate every time I err, so that before long, life will seem unbearable. The solution is to turn to repentance. As Ezekiel tells us: If a wicked person does not acknowledge his sins, he will die, but if he repents and does what is good, he will live.

Common sense dictates that repentance is not a simple process. One cannot just say "I'm sorry" and walk away. Typically, repentance involves four things: (1) taking responsibility for the offending action; (2) making a public confession of guilt—normally before the person one has offended; (3) asking for forgiveness; and (4) making a sincere effort not to repeat the offense. According to Cohen, the taking of responsibility and the confession of guilt can be understood as the punishments one imposes on oneself.[25]

Now comes Ezekiel's great insight as captured by the quotation that opens this chapter: "Cast away all the transgressions by which you offended, and get yourselves a new heart and a new spirit" (18:31). We are not defined by our past mistakes. Provided that we follow the path of repentance, we are free to make ourselves over and start anew. In this way, the act of repentance by which I take control over my own life is the ultimate expression of freedom.

Maimonides too stressed the importance of freedom in his treatise on repentance: "Free will is granted to all men. If one desires to turn himself to the path of good and be righteous, the choice is hers. Should he desire to turn to the path of evil and be wicked, the choice is his. . . . Each person is fit to be righteous like Moses, our teacher, or like Jeroboam. [Similarly] he may be wise or foolish, merciful or cruel, miserly or generous, or [acquire] any other character traits."[26] Which road we take depends on the degree to which we take responsibility for our transgressions and make a concerted effort not to repeat them. Cohen went further, saying that repentance opens up the possibility of self-transformation, and in so doing turns the individual into a fully developed person.[27] That is why, to our sensibilities, the animal sacrifice practiced in ancient times seems artificial: Unlike repentance, it does not force one to come to grips with who one is and what one has done.

To be sure, admitting responsibility for our transgressions and making an effort not to repeat them may be the most difficult thing we are ever asked to do. But difficult or not, it is an essential feature of Jewish thought and practice. A classical Rabbinic text asks us to repent one day before our death.[28] Since we do not know when we will die, the upshot is that we should repent every day of our lives. The same source tells us that one hour of repentance and good deeds on this earth is better than a whole life in the world to come.[29] Yet another says that where the truly repentant stand, not even the perfectly righteous can stand (Berachot 39b).

The last of these sayings underscores Cohen's point that one has to take control of one's life to be a fully developed person. Imagine someone who has never done anything wrong. He does not repent for past sins for the simple reason that he has not committed any. He pays his taxes, tells the truth, gives the requisite amount of money to charity, treats others always with kindness, and never speaks ill of people behind their backs. Therefore, he has never asked to be forgiven. Cohen's point—and the Rabbis' too—is that something important is missing. It is one thing not to sin, another to sin and have the strength of character to admit it and take the necessary steps to overcome it.

Needless to say, the example we are considering is far-fetched. No one goes through life without doing anything wrong. If a person were to believe this about herself, we would write her off as a pompous idiot. That is all the more reason why repentance is so important: It forces us to examine our lives and be honest about what we find. To this Cohen adds one more point. Although repentance involves self-examination, it can never be self-contained. On Yom Kippur, we are asked to reach out to the people we have offended during the previous year. But, Cohen insists, ultimately repentance must be carried out before God because God is the ultimate judge, the one who demands truth, the one who alone looks into our hearts and can tell whether we are being sincere when we say that we will do our best not to repeat the offense.[30]

In the last analysis, then, Cohen says that God is the ultimate source of forgiveness. If we are reconciled with God, then we can reconcile with ourselves.[31] In Ezekiel's words (11:19): "The heart of stone is now replaced by a heart of flesh." Cohen therefore maintains that by stressing the individual's responsibility for her own sin, Ezekiel has also put us on the doorstep of a new conception of God. "The forgiveness of sins," Cohen concludes, "becomes the special and most appropriate function of God's goodness."[32] Or, more fully: "The entire monotheistic worship is based on forgiveness of sin."[33]

Can the Future Affect the Past?

Thus far we have treated past mistakes as unalterable facts. But there is another way of looking at them. In his account of repentance, the great Orthodox theologian Joseph Soloveitchik (1903–93) challenged the idea that the past cannot be changed. From a scientific point of view, it is true that time is linear: If A causes B, then A determines the nature of B, rather than vice versa. Soloveitchik replies, however, that this model does not work for repentance if it is genuine and done out of love rather than out of fear of punishment.[34]

The basis for Soloveitchik's view is a talmudic passage (Yoma 86b) that says the power of repentance is so great that it can turn deliberate sins into meritorious acts. How can this be? The answer is that, properly understood, repentance is creative. In the words of Ezekiel, the person who repents takes on a new heart and a new spirit, which Soloveitchik interprets as meaning different desires, longings, and goals. In effect, the one who repents becomes a different person than he once was, or, as Soloveitchik expresses it, he "creates himself, his own 'I.'"[35] Instead of brooding over a past act that cannot be undone, this person's focus is on the future, which is to say a new and better future.

With this scenario, the future changes our understanding of the past in the sense that what started out as a sin is now seen as a step on the way to a mitzvah, or good deed. As Soloveitchik puts it: "The future transforms the thrust of the past."[36] It is as if B has determined the nature of A. Although backward causation in time is paradoxical in one sense, Soloveitchik insists that it is how repentance works: "A great man can utilize his past sins and transgressions for the sake of achieving great and exalted goals."[37] In an obvious reference to Ezekiel, he concludes by saying that "past aberrations can, at times, descend upon dry bones like the life-giving dew of resurrection."[38]

From the Sixth Century BCE to the Twentieth Century CE

Would Ezekiel have agreed with all of this? Although it may be comforting to say yes, the truth is likely more nuanced. Cohen had the advantage of standing on the shoulders of the Rabbis, Maimonides, and Kant, all of whom advanced the discussion of freedom and responsibility. In addition to philosophy and theology, Cohen was also exposed to Renaissance painting and Romantic poetry, which emphasized the dignity of the individual and the full extent of what the individual could accomplish. It stands to reason that his reading of Ezekiel is selective. Much the same is true of Soloveitchik, who emphasizes the transformative power of repentance to such a degree that it becomes a kind of self-creation.

We saw that Ezekiel's sayings are not always consistent with one another. Granted, he introduced the idea of individual responsibility to Judaism. But did he consider this his most paramount teaching? Was his view of what it means to be an individual the same as Cohen's or

Soloveitchik's? Would he have said that the future can alter the moral significance of the past?

Most likely, the answer to these questions is no because it would have been next to impossible for him to anticipate trends that did not materialize until much later. What is more, we saw that he still believed in the sacrificial cult. And yet, there is something extraordinary about this priest living in Babylonia in the sixth century BCE who had such a lasting impact on the thought of later generations.

This is another way of saying that great literary texts such as the sayings of Ezekiel are not static. In addition to satisfying their contemporary audiences, the real significance of these works is sometimes not known until years, perhaps even centuries, after the author's death. This is as true for Ezekiel as it is for such famous passages from the Torah as Moses' encounter with God at the burning bush (Exod. 3) or God's revelation to Moses on Mount Sinai (Exod. 34). We may conclude that, despite all the controversy that surrounds his prophecy, Ezekiel's significant influence on later generations is reason enough to conclude that he was indeed a prophet tasked with relaying a divine message.

CHAPTER 7

Second Isaiah

Monotheism Takes Hold

I am the first and I am the last;
And there is no god but Me.

—ISAIAH 44:6

This quotation is taken from Second Isaiah, a prophet whose sayings occupy chapters 40–55 of the book of Isaiah. The author, whose real name is unknown, lived after Jerusalem fell to the Babylonians. With the Temple in ruins and much of the nation living in exile, it would have been natural for the people to feel despondent and ask, "Has God forgotten us?" In the face of such despair, Second Isaiah preaches a message of hope and consolation. God has not forgotten Israel. On the contrary, God loves Israel and, in time, will redeem it. Thus the first verse attributed to Second Isaiah reads:

Comfort, oh comfort My people,
Says your God.
Speak tenderly to Jerusalem,
And declare to her
That her term of service is over,
That her iniquity is expiated;
For she has received at the land of the LORD
Double for all her sins. (40:1–2)

As it happens, Babylonia fell to Cyrus of Persia in 539 BCE, after which Cyrus allowed the exiles to return to Jerusalem and practice their religion. Although not everyone chose to return, those who did began work on a Second Temple, which was completed around 515 BCE.

An Explicit Commitment to Monotheism

Second Isaiah is noteworthy for his explicit commitment to monotheism. Although monotheism is often regarded as Judaism's greatest contribution to world culture, like most blockbuster ideas, it did not emerge all at once. Tradition has it that Abraham was the first monotheist and distinguished himself by smashing his father's idols.[1] The truth, however, is that the Torah says nothing about this, and almost nothing about Abraham's theology. Did he think that his God was the only one, or that his God was the most powerful and important one among a group of gods? All we know is that Abraham trusted in God and was willing to sacrifice his son at God's command.

The same ambiguity affects the song the Israelites sing to celebrate safe passage through the Red Sea: "Who is like you, O LORD, *among the gods*?" (Exod. 15:11).[2] At first reading, this verse seems to imply that the God who just rescued Israel from the Egyptian army is one among a number of deities, albeit the most important. While the NJPS translation substitutes "celestials" for "gods," this does little to clear up the issue. Who or what are these celestials? Are they immortal? If so, why should we not consider them gods?

Even the Second Commandment leaves room for doubt. Exodus 20:3–5 proclaims: "You shall have no other gods besides me. You shall not make for yourself a sculptured image, or any likeness of what is in the heavens above, or on the earth below, or in the waters under the earth. You shall not bow down to them or serve them." As discussed in chapter 2, the commandment tells us *that* we should have no other gods before us, but not *why*. Is it because no other gods exist and therefore worship of them amounts to folly, or is it because the true God insists on having our undivided attention? By the same token, the text does not tell us why we cannot make images of God. Is it because it is impossible to capture God's likeness in a piece of wood or stone, or because God does not want to be worshiped by having people bow down to statues? Or is it something else?

Later passages leave us just as puzzled. Exodus 24:10 says quite clearly that Moses, Aaron, and the elders of Israel saw God. Similar sentiments are expressed by First Isaiah (6:1) and Ezekiel (1:26). If a person can see God, especially God in the form of a human being, then one should be able to sculpt an image of God. This implies that the prohibition against doing so is more a matter of divine preference than of metaphysical necessity. On the other hand, Deuteronomy 4:12 says that the people saw no form at Sinai; there was only a voice. This is often taken to mean that God has no form that could be captured in a material medium. Which view is right?

It is not until Second Isaiah that we get the wherewithal to answer some of these questions. In fact, it could be said that he is the first person to see the full import of monotheism. Later thinkers refer back to him when they try to say what monotheism amounts to—in effect, what we are committing ourselves to when we say the *Shema*. We shall see, however, that the doctrine is both more complicated and more controversial than people normally think.

Monotheism: The Basics

Properly understood, monotheism involves two claims: (1) God is the one and only deity who exists, and (2) God is incomparable to anything else. The first claim can be found in the quotation that opens this chapter, when the prophet says that there is no other god but the true one.[3] It is not that the gods recognized by polytheistic religions are inferior to God but that they do not even exist. Accordingly, "See, they are all nothingness, / Their works are nullity, / Their statues are naught and nil" (Isa. 41:29). Note that whereas Hosea saw idolatry as a moral failing comparable to adultery (see chapter 2), for Second Isaiah, idolatry is more the intellectual failing of trusting in a figment of the imagination. He says several times that the statues people have erected to their gods cannot say anything, do anything, or think anything. Thus, anyone who prays to them or bows down to them is basically a fool who "never says to himself, / 'The thing in my hand is a fraud!'" (44:20).

We can see the need for the second claim by recognizing that worship of a God who resembles a human being and whose likeness can be captured in material form—a god such as Zeus or Thor—would not count as monotheistic as we now understand the term. Cohen expresses this point by saying that the issue at stake in monotheism is not so much "oneness" (*einheit*) as "uniqueness" (*einzigheit*).[4] In essence, there is more to monotheism than simple arithmetic. In addition to recognizing only one God, it holds that God is special, in a class to which nothing else belongs.

To understand what is behind Second Isaiah's commitment to uniqueness, recall the wording of the Second Commandment: "You shall not make for yourself a sculptured image, or any likeness of what is in the heavens above, or on the earth below, or in the waters under the earth" (Exod. 20:4). In other words, there is no such thing as a good versus a bad likeness, because they are all doomed from the start.

Second Isaiah expresses this point when he asks, "To whom, then, can you liken God, / What form compare to Him?" (40:18). As he tells us in the same chapter (40:15–17), "The nations are but a drop in a bucket, / Reckoned as dust on a balance; . . . / All nations are as naught in His sight; / He accounts them as less than nothing." This could be understood to extend to the mightiest rulers, warriors, castles, tidal waves, thunderbolts, sea monsters, or heavenly bodies: All are as nothing before God as well. Although mighty in their own way, they are part of the created order, and therefore incomparable to the *creator*.

The biblical scholar Marc Brettler objects that Second Isaiah has gone too far in his criticism of idolatry. After all, people who thought their gods could be represented in material form were not so stupid as to believe that a statue *is* the god, only that the statue *stands for* the god.[5] For example, Zeus was supposed to reside on Mount Olympus, but statues and drawings of him could be found throughout the Greek world. By the same token, the ruler of a country may be represented in pictures installed in public buildings, but no one supposes that the picture *is* the ruler. Nonetheless, it would be natural to suppose that people who show disrespect to the picture also disrespect the ruler, while people who honor the picture honor the ruler. As applied to a god such as Zeus, even if he did not occupy a statue erected in his temple, it could be said that he would take a good deal of interest in how people responded to it.

In defense of Second Isaiah, I submit that a statue can stand for a god only if there is a discernable connection between the two. In most cases, that connection is a physical resemblance. Thus, Zeus, god of the sky and thunder, was often depicted with a muscular torso and a strong, serious facial expression; Aphrodite, the goddess of love, with a gorgeous figure; Marduk, the patron god of Babylonia, as a fearsome snake dragon; and the mother goddess Asherah with protruding breasts. All these representations were intended to convey salient features of the deity and inspire an appropriate response.

Against this, Second Isaiah is telling us that muscles, breasts, body type, or facial expressions have nothing to do with divinity. That is why there is no such thing as a good versus a bad likeness—all are distortions. Ditto for lions, birds, reptiles, or other animals. If he is right, then the statues erected for gods and goddesses are objectionable no matter how much attention they command.

In time, the insights provided by Second Isaiah would play a decisive role in the thought of Maimonides. Like the prophet, Maimonides regarded idolatry as an intellectual error: worshiping a figment of the imagination rather than a genuine reality. At one point, he went so far as to say that the imagination is identical to the evil impulse (*yetzer hara*) in human beings because of its power to draw people away from reality and lead them to the world of make-believe.[6] He went on to say that there is only one way to counter the allure of a make-believe world: to develop the human intellect to its fullest extent. In addition to study of the Torah, he recommended the study of secular subjects such as logic, mathematics, biology, and astronomy. In his view, only a lifetime of learning would prepare one to see how dangerous the imagination can be.

Like Second Isaiah, Maimonides stressed that any comparison between God and humans is faulty. Biblical passages that describe God as having arms or feet, sitting on a throne, descending on Mount Sinai, or displaying bursts of anger are not to be read as literal descriptions but rather as metaphors designed to acquaint readers with some aspect of divinity. For example, if a biblical passage portrays God as sitting on a throne in heaven, it seeks to communicate that God is sovereign of the universe. If it says that God saw what was happening on earth, it seeks to communicate that God knows everything that happens, not that God has sense organs. With respect to knowledge, Maimonides insisted that God's knowledge is incomparable to ours — not only greater than ours, but of an entirely different order. If humans gain knowledge by observing things external to ourselves, as the creator of heaven and earth, God has knowledge by looking within the divine self.

With his usual tendency to carry insights to their logical conclusion, Maimonides went on to maintain that it is *not* true that God is wiser than we are, more powerful than we are, better than we are, or will last longer than we will.[7] Why not? Because to say that God is wiser than we are implies that there exists a common measure of comparison — as if God has a higher IQ score than we do. Such a comparison — indeed *any* comparison — conflicts with Second Isaiah's insight by violating the principle of divine uniqueness. Casting an image of God in stone violates this principle at a rudimentary level. Maimonides' point is that we also violate it if all we do is form an image of God in our minds. Like a figure carved in stone, a mental image is a distortion.

If we accept Maimonides' interpretation, then we have a difficult task ahead of us if we are going to be true monotheists. In particular, we have to accustom ourselves to think in conceptual rather than pictorial terms. That is why he stressed the need to study logic, mathematics, biology, and astronomy. As with Second Isaiah, one could object that Maimonides has gone too far. Putting aside relatively easy cases such as passages that describe God as having arms, feet, or sitting on a throne, certain passages (particularly those early on in the Bible) do imply that God occupies space and sometimes takes on human form. To understand what is at stake, we must proceed to the next level.

If, as Second Isaiah claims, God is the only deity and nothing else can be compared to God, then the prophet is asking us to look at the world on the basis of two completely separate categories: God and the created order. Nothing in the created order, whether on earth, in the sea below, or the heavens above, resembles God or can stand as a rival to God. If it weren't for God, the created order would not even exist. If the mightiest of the mighty are as nothing before God, then the line between God and the created order is absolute.

This worldview contrasts sharply with that of mythology, where the line between the divine and the human is crossed all the time. Mighty kings or great warriors become gods, and gods descend to earth to have sexual relations with humans. Second Isaiah is telling us that the mythological way of looking at things is wrong. Nothing can pass from one category to another or straddle the fence between them. As clear as this distinction may be to us, several passages in the Bible seem to ignore it. Genesis 6, which tells of sons of gods having sexual relations with mortal women and producing offspring called Nephilim (often translated as "giants"), is a good example. Although this passage may belong to an old, mythological tradition, it is hardly the only one that could be cited. The Nephilim are mentioned at Numbers 13:33 and Ezekiel 32:27 as well. Furthermore, as the biblical scholar James Kugel has shown, our ancestors did not always view the spiritual as something that occupies a separate realm but rather as something capable of entering our realm.[8] According to this view, nothing would prevent God from taking on human form and talking to people in the same way that people talk to one another.

The most prominent example of God taking on human form can be found at Genesis 18:1–14, when God suddenly appears to Abraham at the oak trees of Mamre. As Abraham looks up, he sees three strange men standing near him. He prepares a meal for them and learns that they know the name of his wife. In fact, one of the visitors predicts that Sarah, who is past childbearing age, will give birth to a child in the following year. Sarah laughs, but then something remarkable happens. Without any warning, God speaks and says that nothing is too difficult for God to do. This has led many commentators to speculate that one of the three visitors who came to Abraham was in fact God in human form.

A similar episode is reported at Genesis 21:15–19, when an angel speaks to Hagar in the desert. At first the angel speaks of God in the third person, saying that God has heard Ishmael's voice, but then, without warning, the text shifts to the first person: "I will make a great nation of him." This seems to imply that the angel has somehow morphed into God. Later, at Genesis 32:24–30, we learn that Jacob wrestles with an angel during the night. But when dawn breaks, he names the place where this occurred *Peniel* (the face of God), indicating that he has actually struggled with God.[9] At Exodus 3:2, an angel appears to Moses out of the burning bush—but once again, with no warning, the text (3:6) shifts into the first person; God speaks to Moses directly, saying "I am the God of your father." Finally, there is Judges 6:11–23, where an angel appears to Gideon while he is hiding from the Midianites. First the angel speaks of God in the third person; immediately thereafter the text shifts to the first person: "The Lord said to him, 'I will be with you.'"

With these passages in mind, Kugel argues that God can crop up anywhere and speak to a person whenever God determines it is advisable to do so.[10] In other passages, God, or a manifestation of God, seems to enter the earthly realm and occupy space. The most prominent of these is Exodus 40:34, which says that the glory (*kavod*) of God filled the Tabernacle so that Moses could not enter it. Admittedly, it is difficult to pinpoint exactly what is meant by the glory of God in this context.[11] Elsewhere in the Bible the expression refers to God or to something intimately connected to God—sometimes to a blinding light that emanates from God, and sometimes to the honor or respect due to God. Despite this ambiguity, it is likely that much of the original audience took the passage to mean that God had taken up physical location because God's glory prevented Moses from occupying the same place.

The same ambiguity applies to the Rabbinic concept of God's indwelling presence or *Shekhinah*. At Exodus 25:8 God says, "Let them make Me a sanctuary that I may dwell among them." The Rabbis took the biblical Hebrew word for "dwell" (*shakhon*) and converted it into the noun *Shekhinah* (which itself never appears in the Bible). Like the glory of God, the *Shekhinah* in Rabbinic literature is said to shine down on earth and occupy space.[12] Sometimes the *Shekhinah* is said to take on human characteristics, such as feeling pain, shedding tears, or crossing back into the heavenly realm.[13] Any time you turn a verb into a noun, you create the impression that the noun is a thing or separate entity in its own right. What does it mean to say that God is present to a person or group of people? Is it that God has crossed the line and entered the created order? Is it that an offshoot of God, what theologians call a "hypostasis," has crossed the line?[14] Or, once again, is there some other possibility?

As indicated above, monotheism did not emerge all at once. What distinguishes Second Isaiah is his insistence that the line separating God and everything else is inviolate. Separation does not mean that God takes no interest in what happens in the created order—quite the contrary—but that the crea*tor* remains unlike anything in the crea*tion*. Like most of the prophets, he uses anthropomorphic language to describe God. For example, at 41:10 and 41:13, he speaks of God's hand; at 44:3 he says that God pours water on thirsty soil. As discussed in chapter 2, though, the Bible often uses metaphorical language to drive home a point. In no sense do these passages compromise his commitment to divine uniqueness and exclusivity.

Monotheism versus Powerful Human Instincts

Still, the monotheistic view of the world presents a challenge. As Heschel articulated: "Monotheism is at variance with powerful human instincts."[15] These instincts reduce to two: (1) the belief that the only things we can trust are those we can see or put our hands on, and (2) the belief that in times of crisis or misfortune, we can find a simple way to curry favor with God. Put the two together and you get the desire to identify a visible or tangible thing that does straddle the fence.

The list of proposed fence-straddlers is long and varied. The most obvious candidates are the heavenly bodies, which appear to occupy a midpoint between heaven and earth. For millennia, people all over the world believed that the position of the stars and planets had a decisive effect on human destiny. If you studied the zodiac carefully enough, it was thought, you could decipher what God intended for crop cycles, military engagements, political campaigns, stock market movements, love affairs—in fact, almost anything one could name.

Many Jews used the zodiac to predict when the Messiah would come. The ancient historian Josephus writes that misinterpretation of astrological signs was one of the causes inciting Israel to revolt against Rome.[16] The talmudic tractate *Shabbat* 53b says that every person is born under the protection of a star. Later (156a) it says that the planets determine the character of the people born under them, so that a person born under the protection of Jupiter will be just while one born under the protection of Mars will spill blood. Gersonides (1288–1344), a prominent Jewish philosopher and scientist in his day, believed that heavenly bodies control the thoughts and actions of people.[17] Numerous references to astrological phenomena appear in Shakespeare's plays, showing that whether or not he believed in astrology himself, he must have been well versed in its theory and methods.[18]

Against all of this, Maimonides argued some eight hundred years ago that astrology has no scientific basis and is just another form of idolatry.[19] Although he studied the movement of the stars and planets and believed in the existence of disembodied heavenly intelligences, he held that just like everything else in the created order, the stars and planets are not worthy of worship, and there is no reason to turn to them for guidance.

Another obvious candidate for fence-straddlers are angels. In the Torah, angels come down to earth, talk to people, and carry messages from God. For example, an angel tells Abraham not to lay a hand on Isaac at Genesis 22. Like their Christian counterparts, Jewish art and literature contain elaborate angelologies. Although the ancient Rabbis debate when the angels were created (*Genesis Rabbah* 1.3), the important point is that they were created at all and thus not eternal. Although it is customary to think of angels as perfect, sometimes in Rabbinic literature they are portrayed as jealous or short-sighted.[20] With minor exceptions (e.g., a night prayer and the *Shalom Aleichem* hymn), no prayers are directed to them.[21] In fact, a talmudic source (*J. Berachot* 9.13a.) has God say: "If trouble befall someone, let him not cry to Michael or Gabriel; let him cry to Me and I will answer him." In the traditional Passover Haggadah God famously says: "I will pass through the land of Egypt: I Myself and not an angel. And I will smite every firstborn: I Myself and not a Seraph. And on all the gods of Egypt I will execute judgment: I Myself and not a messenger. I, the Eternal, I am the One, and none other." Needless to say, "I and none other" echoes the words of Second Isaiah.

Just below the angels stands Moses, who, according to Exodus 33:11, speaks to God "face to face." Earlier on (20:16), he is asked to intercede between the people and God because the people are too afraid to go near the mountain on which God has descended. Nonetheless, Moses is prohibited from entering the Promised Land. No prayers are addressed to him, and despite his major role in the Exodus, no traditional Haggadah mentions him. We are never told where he died, so that to this day, there is no possibility of erecting a temple or shrine to commemorate his death.

Less exalted than angels and heavenly bodies are magical names, magical numbers, rabbit's feet, four-leaf clovers, silver bullets, crystal balls, and a host of other things thought to possess occult powers. We can well imagine God saying that, in times of need, we should not turn to these things either. The same applies to religious implements like *Kiddush* cups, *kippot*, tefillin, or *mezuzot*. Aside from their aesthetic or historical value, these objects serve an important function: They help us to perform rituals that direct our attention to God. To the degree that they do this, they deserve respect — not as good luck charms, but as implements of worship. For example, a mezuzah serves as a reminder that we have pledged to think about, obey, and teach God's commandments. But, left to its own devices, it has no power to protect someone from sickness or misfortune. In the words of Second Isaiah, it is the work of human craftsmen. To endow it with special powers would be to treat it as an idol.

Last but not least are people in high places. In the ancient world, the pharaohs of Egypt and some of the emperors of Rome were worshiped as living gods. In our world, movie stars, athletes, political figures, and, in some cases, religious leaders, demand and often receive adulation from their followers. If adulation leads to the belief that these people are demi-gods that straddle the fence between the divine and the human, then idolatry has reemerged. In the words of the scholar and educator Rabbi Solomon Schechter: The establishment of an intermediary is really the setting up of another god and hence the cause of sin.[22]

Monotheism through the Ages

Perhaps there is no better gloss on Second Isaiah's claim that everything is as nothing before God than the twentieth-century philosopher Emmanuel Levinas's observation that what Judaism has done is to de-charm the world.[23] This does not mean that one cannot take pleasure in a sunrise, gaze at the stars in wonder, or admire the size and majesty of a redwood tree. It means instead that these things are part of a natural order that owes its existence and its power to something else. Gone are the days when local deities inhabited rivers, forests, or mountain tops, when magical incantations could turn pieces of wood into objects of worship, when people searched the entrails of birds for clues about human destiny. It was the Hebrew prophets, and most importantly Second Isaiah, who taught the world that all of this is folly.

More than 2,500 years separate Levinas from Second Isaiah. But the difference in time should not deter us from seeing that they are allies in a war against illusion and superstition. Heschel is right to say that the enemy is formidable. Jewish folklore still ascribes magical powers to the Ark of the Covenant, amulets, curses, demons, and magical numbers. Perhaps the best rallying cry in this struggle are Second Isaiah's words: "The thing in my hand is a fraud!" So, too, we might add: the thing before my eyes or dancing around in my imagination.

No doubt problems can arise when we try to apply sayings from past ages to our lives today. The Torah asks Israel to fight a bitter war against the gods of other nations. Thus Deuteronomy 7:5 says that when the

Israelites enter the land God is giving them, they should break down the altars of the native population, smash their pillars, hew down their sacred poles, and burn their idols. Throughout the Rabbinic period and the Middle Ages, Jewish authorities debated whether Christianity counted as idolatry. Although nothing was known about Buddhism, Hinduism, or Taoism, we can well imagine people asking the same questions about them. In a pluralistic society like ours today, these views have to be modified. Similarly, although the Rabbis went to great lengths to insulate Jews from what they perceived as the idolatry of the Greco-Roman world, few people today would argue that modern Jews should ignore the art and literature of this period.

To this point, we can note that even in antiquity, the door to religious pluralism was not entirely shut. Rabbi Joshua is famous for saying that the righteous of every nation will have a share in the world to come; in other words, even non-Jews can attain salvation (*Tosefta Sanhedrin* 13:2). Granted, he probably understood "righteous" (*tzaddikim*) to refer to gentiles who abided by the seven Noahide Laws, one of which prohibits idolatrous worship. Still, nothing prevents us from taking "righteous" in a broader sense to include people who live a morally upright life.[24] This parallels the opinion of the famous medieval Rabbi Menachem Meiri (1249–1306), who thought that "idolatry" referred to ancient cults that tolerated or encouraged lawless or immoral behavior, not to Christianity or Islam.[25] Maimonides was steeped in Islamic thought, and readily acknowledged his debt to it. He also acknowledged his debt to Aristotle, a pagan. Cohen, Martin Buber, and Franz Rosenzweig all learned from Christianity. Finally, there is the view of Heschel, who wrote that God's voice speaks in many languages.[26] We can admit all of this, be tolerant of other religions, and still maintain that Judaism stands on the insights that Second Isaiah articulated.

CHAPTER 8

Job

Innocent Suffering

He wounds me much for no cause.
He does not let me catch my breath,
But sates me with bitterness. . . .
It is all one; therefore I say,
"He destroys the blameless and the guilty." . . .
He mocks as the innocent fail.
The earth is handed over to the wicked one;
He covers the eyes of its judges.
If it is not He, then who?

—JOB 9:17–24

The question stemming from the "problem of evil" has plagued some of the greatest human minds since ancient times. In its classic formulation, it goes as follows: If God is all knowing, then God is aware that innocent people suffer. If God is all good, then God must not want innocent people to suffer. If God is all powerful, then God is capable of preventing innocent suffering. Why, then, do innocent people suffer?

One easy solution is to say that God does not exist. A second easy solution is to say that there is no such thing as innocent suffering. In other words, since God is all good, just, and merciful, all who suffer deserve what they get, or will be compensated for their troubles at some future time. To my way of thinking, both of these solutions are facile, and one of the merits of the book of Job is that it shows us why.

The Story and Its Questions

Although the storyline of the book of Job is simple, there are a number of sudden turns and enigmatic speeches. The prologue says that Job is a blameless and upright man who fears God and shuns evil. He has seven sons and three daughters and has acquired great wealth. When God says to Satan that Job is a faithful servant, Satan replies that he has good reason to be: look at all God has done for him.[1] What if all that he has is suddenly taken away? Would he remain faithful or become despondent and curse God?

Upon hearing this, God allows Satan to take away all that Job has but not to touch Job himself. Soon thereafter Job learns that all his children have perished and all his livestock have been carried off in a violent storm. Though Job is distraught, he does not curse God. Instead he utters the famous line (1:21): "The LORD has given, and the LORD has taken away; blessed be the name of the LORD." Again, God tells Satan that Job is a faithful servant. Undaunted, Satan says that if he could touch Job himself, then Job would in fact curse God. God decides to allow Satan to afflict Job but not to take his life. Satan proceeds to afflict Job head to toe with painful sores. Although his wife asks him to curse God and die as a way of ending his suffering, he refuses.

Three friends, Eliphaz, Bildad, and Zophar, then come to comfort him. Much of the book is taken up with their speeches and Job's replies. As the story progresses, the friends propose versions of the second easy solution mentioned above: There is no such thing as innocent suffering. For example, at 4:7 Eliphaz asks: "What innocent man ever perished?" But as the reader knows, and Job continues to insist, they are mistaken. Job has done nothing to deserve his fate.

Rejecting the advice of his friends at 9:17–24, Job accuses God of wronging him ("He wounds me much for no cause"); of paying no attention to innocence or guilt ("He destroys the blameless and the guilty"); and of showing favor to the guilty ("The earth is handed over to the wicked one"). Above all, he continues to proclaim his innocence: "Until I die I will maintain my integrity. / I will persist in my righteousness and will not yield; / I shall be free of reproach as long as I live" (27:5–6). From this point on, we don't hear from the friends again. After they leave the story, Elihu, a younger friend, enters it and delivers a long discourse on divine providence ("Surely it is false that God does not listen") and urges Job to submit to God's superior wisdom ("The case is before Him; / So wait for Him") (35:13–14). Job listens but does not answer.

Then God appears again and addresses Job out of a whirlwind. "Who is this who darkens counsel, / Speaking without knowledge?" (38:2).[2] God asks a series of rhetorical questions intended to belittle Job's importance: Where were you when the earth was formed? Can you measure it? Have you plumbed the depths of the sea? Have you seen the gates of the netherworld? Can you order the heavenly bodies?

Finally Job answers God in a spirit of remorse, indicating that he spoke without understanding and recants what he said (42:4–6,). Exactly what Job is recanting is unclear. Is he now denying that God lets innocent people suffer? Or that God lets innocents suffer more than the guilty? Or that he is even in a position to question God? All we know is that Job repents and says nothing more.

In the epilogue, God does not respond directly to Job, and never mentions the wager with Satan. Rather, God proceeds to criticize Job's friends, saying they did not speak the truth, whereas Job did. Again, we are not told which truths or untruths these are. Following this, God restores Job's fortunes twice over, doubling what he had before.

Clearly, the story leaves a number of questions unanswered. Why would a just and merciful God enter a wager with Satan that will afflict harm on an upright man? Why doesn't God answer Job's question about innocent suffering? What point is the story trying to make by having Job repent after hearing God speak? What point is it trying to make by having Job be rewarded twice over in the end?

Our sense of puzzlement is all the more pronounced because the book does not appear to be the product of a single author but an assemblage compiled by different authors with differing points of view. The prologue and epilogue are written in prose, the middle sections in poetry. Some commentators think the prologue is a later addition because the story of God's wager with Satan offers a credible explanation for Job's suffering and therefore exonerates God. This interpretation is consistent with God's failure to mention the wager with Satan when answering Job later on. While the reader is informed of God's reason for allowing Job to suffer, Job himself never is.[3] Other commentators think the epilogue is a later addition because it provides a happy ending to the story and restores faith in divine justice.

The prologue and epilogue are not the only passages that raise questions of authorship. Zophar's third speech is missing. Job's speeches at 24:18–25 and 27:13–23 sound more like the view of his friends, since they seem to say that the wicked are punished after all. Chapter 28 is not attributed to anyone and reads like a freestanding poem. The fact that Elihu does not appear until three-quarters of the way through the book has led many biblical scholars to believe his oration is also a later addition. Because God's speech from the whirlwind completely avoids the question of innocent suffering, some scholars suspect that it too was added later on.

There are even problems with translation. It has not escaped the notice of scholars that when the Bible was translated into Greek, the Job who appears in that text is not nearly as rebellious as the one who appears in the original Hebrew.[4] For Christians (James 5:11), Job is a model of patience or endurance who is rewarded by God for his perseverance in times of distress. But as the biblical scholar Marvin Pope remarks, this view ignores more than nine-tenths of the book and is based only on the prologue and epilogue.[5] In fact, the Hebrew text presents a more complicated figure than the ever-patient Job. For example, the oft-quoted remark of 13:15 ("Though He slay me, yet I will trust in Him") says something quite different in Hebrew. According to the NJPS translation: "He may well slay me; I may have no hope."[6]

By the same token, Job's reply to God at 42:6 has long been disputed.[7] The NJPS translation renders it: "Therefore, I recant and relent, / Being but dust and ashes." But as the commentary points out, we are not told what Job is recanting, and the Hebrew cannot support the phrase "Being but dust and ashes." The Christian New Revised Standard Version has "Therefore I despise myself, / and repent in dust and ashes." But it points out in its commentary that "repent" should not be understood as repentance for a sin, but rather as a change of heart.

Though it is clear that Job is confessing some kind of resignation in the face of God, it is not clear that he is admitting guilt. The uncertainty over Job's status carries over to Rabbinic literature too. According to one interpretation, Job, like Abraham, feared God, but unlike Abraham, his fear was not coupled with love.[8] According to another, Job did serve God out of love.[9] As to Job's anger at God and near blasphemy, one rabbi defended Job by saying that a person is not responsible for things said under duress.[10]

All these difficulties raise an obvious question: What is this book trying to teach us? If it has an answer to the problem of innocent suffering, what is it? If it does not, what are we supposed to do when we see it or experience it ourselves? It is to these questions that we now turn.

Blasphemy or Legitimate Protest?

In assessing the nature of Job's protest, it is important to remember that the Hebrew prophets enjoyed greater latitude in their relation to God than people generally suppose.[11] Abraham did not stand idly by when God threatened to destroy Sodom and Gomorrah; nor did Moses when God threatened to destroy the entire Israelite nation. According to a famous Rabbinic interpretation, Moses grabbed on to God's cloak and would not let go until God forgave Israel.[12] In fact, the idea that God can be held to account by humans is a recurrent theme in biblical literature. We have already encountered the protest of Jeremiah (12:1):

You will win, O LORD, if I make claim against You,
Yet I shall present charges against You:
Why does the way of the wicked prosper?
Why are the workers of treachery at ease?

Similar words are spoken by the prophet Habakkuk (1:2):

How long, O LORD, shall I cry out
And You not listen,
Shall I shout to You, "Violence!"
And You not save?[13]

In these prophets' minds, something is wrong with God's rule of the world. It is not only that innocent people suffer but, in these cases, that guilty people do not. Importantly, these and other such protests are not considered blasphemous. In fact, it may be that God *wants* people to protest when questions about justice are on the line, given that God backs down after listening to Abraham and Moses. It is in this light that we should approach the protests of Job.

The Protests of Job

On the one hand, Job's speeches contain moments of great devotion. Note how closely the following lines (9:2–10) resemble God's speech from the whirlwind at 38–39:

Indeed I know that it is so:
Man cannot win a suit against God.
If he insisted on a trial with Him,
He would not answer one charge in a thousand.
Wise of heart and mighty in power—
Who ever challenged Him and came out whole?—
Him who moves mountains without their knowing it,
Who overturns them in His anger;
Who shakes the earth from its place,
Till its pillars quake;
Who commands the sun not to shine;
Who seals up the stars;
Who by Himself spread out the heavens,

And trod on the back of the sea;
Who made the Bear and Orion,
Pleiades, and the chambers of the south wind;
Who performs great deeds which cannot be fathomed,
And wondrous things without number.

Still, Job does evince other reactions, some of which could be characterized as rebellious:

Doubt: "Would that I knew how to reach Him" (23:5).
Despair: "I am blameless—I am distraught; / I am sick of life"
    (9:20–21).
Self-Pity: "Pity me, pity, You are my friends" (19:21).
Defiance: "It is all one; therefore I say, / He destroys the
    blameless and the guilty" (9:22).

Though Job utters these words under duress, they are nonetheless authentic reactions to his plight. Why, indeed, should Job have to suffer so that God can prove a point to Satan? The book does not provide a direct answer to this question. Rather than discuss the problem of innocent suffering in the abstract, it exhibits the thoughts and feelings of an innocent person in pain. This is another way of saying that the book deals with suffering at a human rather than a theoretical level. As the biblical scholar Jon Levenson points out, the overwhelming tendency of writers as they confront undeserved evil is not to explain it away, but to call on God to take it away.[14] The question, then, is not "Why is there evil?" but "How should one respond to evil?"

It is therefore a mistake to concentrate on humility or rebellion alone and fail to see that both are legitimate responses to the situation. A completely humble Job would close his eyes to what he perceives as injustice and accept whatever God hands out. A completely rebellious Job would feel nothing in the way of reverence. Neither is true to the character in the book, and it is important to see why.

The word "theodicy" derives from the Greek *theos* (God) + *dike* (justice) and means the vindication of God's goodness in a world that appears to contain evil and suffering. Thus theodicy tries to show that there is a reason why God allows evil and suffering to occur. Philosophers and theologians have proposed numerous and varied explanations, including suffering is needed now so that we will better appreciate goodness later on; suffering and evil are needed to give us the opportunity to rise above them; the suffering of some people is needed to achieve a greater and more inclusive good for others; suffering may seem unjustified now, but eventually the innocent will be rewarded and the guilty punished; and finally because we are all sinners, we all deserve to suffer.

There are, of course, circumstances in which some of these explanations are true. Many parents would gladly suffer if it meant their children would be better off as a result. A martyr may undergo suffering to call attention to social ills. Recall that Jeremiah knew he would suffer if he carried the word of God to Jerusalem. Note, however, that these examples involve a choice and are directed to a purpose, whereas Job is never given a choice and never told why he is suffering. In general the problem with theodicy is that it treats every instance of suffering as justifiable, so that even when a child is stricken with cancer or people are killed at a mass shooting, it assures us that all is well with the world.

Though it may provide solace, the trouble with theodicy is that also leads to complacency. Against this, Kant argues that theodicy represents a case where the intended defense (of God) is worse than the original charge.[15] As discussed in relation to the Holocaust in chapter 3, it is unacceptable to say that the murder of innocent children serves a higher purpose. With this sort of consideration in mind, Kant concludes that theodicy should be detested by anyone with the slightest spark of morality.

Nowhere is this truer than in the book of Job. Called upon to comfort a sick and bereaved man, Job's friends do exactly the opposite. In fact, their "comfort" is more like an indictment. Suffering, they argue, is the consequence of sin; therefore, if Job is in pain, he must have transgressed somewhere along the line—if not openly, then secretly. Their charge flies in the face of God's assertion in the prologue that Job is a blameless and upright man who fears God and shuns evil (1:8). It also explains why God is angry with the friends in the epilogue.

As the book develops, the indictments against Job become ever more severe. By chapter 22, Eliphaz tells Job that his iniquities have no limit, that he has committed some of the most egregious sins imaginable, including everything from stripping clothes from the needy to assaulting widows and orphans. The fact that neither Eliphaz nor anyone else has seen such behavior from Job is irrelevant: It is required by the view that suffering is always a punishment for sin.

So Kant is right: Here, theodicy has gotten in the way of Eliphaz's seemingly natural feelings of compassion toward his friend. Otherwise, Job's suffering would have become his suffering. Earlier Job had told him that if their situations were reversed, "I would encourage you with words, / My moving lips would bring relief" (16:5). It is not that Eliphaz is incapable of empathy. The problem is, he has committed himself to a theodicy at odds with the facts before him. In the end, because he cannot feel compassion for his friend, Eliphaz comes across as contemptible.

Similarly compelled to face the facts, Job's two other friends try out a number of diversions. Suffering brings one closer to God (5:17). No person is truly innocent (25:4–6). God is such a mystery that we cannot know anything (11:6–8). Yet these responses effectively belittle the seriousness of Job's predicament. Blatantly missing is a sense of outrage: How horrible! How could this happen, especially to you! We need to do something! None of the friends seems troubled by Job's predicament or willing to plead on his behalf. Job's comment that "the upright are amazed at this" (17:8), meaning that decent people would be disturbed by the sight of an innocent person in pain, also fails to elicit empathy. We have seen that Abraham, Moses, and Jeremiah all spoke out when they thought they saw injustice. The friends resort to theodicy.

What is more, the friends never come to grips with the essential question Job has posed: How can a just and merciful God allow this to happen?

It is important to recognize that Job never denies the existence of God. On the contrary, it is *because* God exists and is just and merciful that he cannot make sense of his situation. Without such a God, there would be no court in which to argue his case (9:15–16, 13:20–23, 23:1–6), no avenger (*goel*, 19:25) to right his wrong.[16] The issue, then, is not "Is there a God?" but rather "Why has God not acted to right an obvious wrong?" As Job says at 13:24: "Why do You hide Your face, / And treat me like an enemy?"

When Job finally encounters God in the voice from the whirlwind, there is no mention of theodicy—on Job's part or God's. This may seem confusing to some readers because, like Job's friends, they are so committed to theodicy that its absence from God's speech has led them to think the speech must not be genuine. If the various attempts at theodicy are sound, how could God *not* invoke them? But let us ask: What would be gained had God had answered Job the way these people would have wished? Suppose God had said that Job's suffering is needed to realize a greater or more inclusive good. Would his plight be any more bearable?

I suggest that it would not. In my view, it would only allow another generation of "comforters" to look human misery in the face and explain it away. Not only does God not resort to theodicy, God expresses anger at those who do—Eliphaz and the other friends (42:7). Note too that God never refers to "chastisements of love," the view that God metes out punishment as a corrective intended to make us better people. In fact, God never generalizes from Job's suffering to anyone else's.

According to the theologian Rabbi Robert Gordis, God does not deny that there is innocent suffering—and in some passages, for example, 40:9–14, where God basically says to Job "See if you can do any better," comes close to admitting it.[17] What is more, in the prologue (2:3), God admits that Satan has inflicted suffering on Job "for no good reason." If a solution to the problem of evil means that we must find some good in every instance of pain, then, I submit, a solution cannot and should not be found.

At this point, it would appear that the book leads us into a dilemma. On the one hand, we are shown the inhumane consequences of appealing to theodicy. On the other hand, we are encouraged to regard Job's plight as unjust. We, too, want to know why a blameless and God-fearing man is now sitting on an ash heap with sores all over his body. How does the book help to resolve this tension?

Although God's response to Job may not offer much in the way of comfort, there is no question that it changes the tenor of the discussion. The man who protests loudly against God now withdraws in chapter 42 on the grounds that he has spoken of things too great for him to understand. Has he been intimidated by the thunder of God's voice? A more charitable explanation would be that Job experiences awe both in the face of God and the vast, mysterious universe God describes to him:

> Where were you when I laid the earth's foundations? . . .
> Have you ever commanded the day to break, . . .
> Have you penetrated to the sources of the sea,
> Or walked in the recesses of the deep? . . .
> Have you surveyed the expanses of the earth? . . .
> Can you tie the cords to Pleiades
> Or undo the reins of Orion? (38:4–31)

Maimonides thought this explanation was enough. In his interpretation, Job is called righteous at the beginning of the story, but not wise. After God's speech, Job gains wisdom by coming to see that the things he valued before—health, wealth, friends—are of little account. Now, he sees what really matters: the greatness of God and God's creation, as well as the smallness of his own place within it.[18]

While this interpretation has some textual support, we should keep in mind that it is based on a controversial premise: Theoretical wisdom is the only thing in life valuable as an end in itself. There is no question that Maimonides himself believed this. The subject at issue is whether this is the point the story is trying to make. I find it hard to agree with Maimonides in large part because his reading plays down the importance of the rebellious Job, and with it the indignation we feel on his behalf. Does Job's insistence that his plight is unfair completely give way to his acceptance of the smallness of his position? It is to this question that we now turn.

When their theodicies begin to crumble, Job's friends question the efficacy of human knowledge and take refuge in a form of skepticism. At 8:9 Bildad says that humans "are of yesterday and know nothing." Later, foreshadowing God's final speech to Job, he says:

> Would you discover the mystery of God?
> Would you discover the limit of the Almighty?
> Higher than heaven—what can you do?
> Deeper than Sheol—what can you know? (11:7–8)

So, too, Elihu counsels:

> Stop to consider the marvels of God.
> Do you know what charge God lays upon them
> When His lightning-clouds shine?
> Do you know the marvels worked upon the expanse of clouds
> By Him whose understanding is perfect? (37:14–16)

Job utters similar sentiments himself in the disputed speech of chapter 28:

> But whence does wisdom come?
> Where is the source of understanding?
> It is hidden from the eyes of all living, . . .
> God understands the way to it;
> He knows its source;
> For He sees to the ends of the earth,
> Observes all that is beneath the heavens. (28:20–24)

Strictly speaking, this sort of skepticism is incompatible with most attempts at theodicy, which claims that divine justice *can* be inferred by looking at earthly events. If, on the other hand, human wisdom is as limited as these passages say—if, when it comes to God's final purpose, we know nothing at all—how can we infer anything?

We saw that when God speaks in the epilogue (38:2), the limits of human knowledge come into play again with the question "Who is this who darkens counsel, / Speaking without knowledge?" In fact, God is not above sarcasm, because some of the questions put to Job are followed up with the taunt, "for surely you know." The picture that emerges from God's speech is that of a universe in which an omnipotent ruler controls terrifying forces that defy human comprehension and dwarf human capability. At 40:15–24, God refers to a monstrous creature called Behemoth, whose bones are like tubes of bronze and whose limbs are like iron rods—a description is followed by the claim: "Only his Maker can draw the sword against him" (40:19).

Shortly thereafter God refers to Leviathan, a creature so frightening that flames shoot from its mouth and even divine beings are afraid of him (42:13–17). The God who has made these creatures and exercises control over them asks Job: "Would you impugn My justice? / Would you condemn Me that you may be right?" (40:8). What is Job supposed to say in the face of such a challenge? Of course, his knowledge and power are as nothing when compared to God's. Hence the reply: "I spoke without understanding / Of things beyond me, which I did not know" (42:3).

An easy lesson to draw from Job's reply is that because we have no comprehension of what it is like to control natural forces on a cosmic scale, all we can do is submit to divine rule, whatever it may involve. But, I admit that this, too, is overly simplistic. Although the humble Job who acknowledges divine sovereignty may replace the angry Job who demands an explanation of innocent suffering, simple humility is not the end of the story.

Both are replaced in the epilogue by Job the prophet. Like other prophets before and after him, Job has experienced God speaking directly to him—and furthermore, despite Job's earlier protests, God acknowledges that Job spoke the truth and continues to refer to him as a servant. This puts Job in a class with Abraham, Moses, and Jeremiah. While all three trust in the saving power of God, they also dispute certain divine decrees. Their relationship with God allows for questioning, arguing, pleading—in short, whatever is necessary to uphold the cause of justice as they understand it.

We also see Job the prophet in how he responds to his friends throughout the course of the book. Had Job listened to his friends, he would have thrown himself on the ground, confessed to sins he did not commit, and begged for mercy. One might argue that a little servility, even an omission of guilt, never hurts in the face of misfortune. And yet, in defiance of everything he has heard from his friends, Job stands up like a hero and speaks the truth:

> As long as there is life in me,
> And God's breath is in my nostrils,
> My lips will speak no wrong,
> Nor my tongue utter deceit. (27:3–4)

It is significant that while God rebukes Job for speaking about cosmic forces he does not understand, God never rebukes him for proclaiming his innocence. The challenge, then, is to see how Job can maintain his moral integrity at the same time that he admits his intellectual fallibility.

Kant argues that when Job humbles himself before God, he is confessing not that he has spoken sacrilegiously, but that he has spoken unwisely about things beyond his comprehension.[19] According to Kant, humans cannot infer God's intentions by looking at earthly events. Good people sometimes suffer, and bad people sometimes flourish. Job's friends are the ones who falsely assume that every aspect of human experience must be in harmony with God's wishes. Citing Job's speech at 27:3–4, Kant takes an opposing position to Maimonides: "Hence only sincerity of heart and not distinction of insight; honesty in openly admitting one's doubts; repugnance to pretending conviction where one feels none, especially before God. . . . These are the attributes which, in the person of Job, have decided the preeminence of the honest man over the religious flatterer in the divine verdict."[20]

For Kant, then, Job's faith is founded on the uprightness of his heart, rather than on his knowledge of God and the cosmos. Kant's interpretation presumes that morality, not theoretical wisdom, is the most valuable thing in human life. In the last analysis, though, Kant's Job is still a version of the patient hero who endures pain with stoic resolution. Still, Kant is right to call attention to Job's honesty. Unlike Eliphaz, who accuses Job of crimes he did not commit and argues that God would never let an innocent person suffer, Job does not try to flatter God by asserting that all is well with the world. Instead, like the other prophets, he finds much that is wrong with the world and says so without hesitation.

In my reading, Job's great virtue is twofold: honesty *coupled with* righteous indignation. Though he repents in the end, this does not negate his protest against innocent suffering earlier on nor his conviction that theodicy is bogus. Looking at the book as a whole, he is both a servant of God and an adversary who takes it on himself to question God. Abraham, Moses, and Jeremiah served as adversaries too, but they were not protesting injustice done to *them*. Instead of seeing honesty and indignation cancel each other out, it would be better to see them together, each legitimate in its own way. In the end, Job can view his suffering in a larger context, but this does not mean that his suffering was justified. To repeat: Even God admits that Job suffered for no good reason.

Limitations and Lessons

As we have seen, the book of Job offers no answer to the question "Why does God permit innocent people to suffer?" It tells us only that we are a small part of a large and often terrifying universe overseen by an omnipotent creator. If anything, modern science has shown that the universe is much larger and even more terrifying than anything biblical authors could have imagined.

Still, I believe our study of Job has left us with other vital lessons. The customary theodicies that people use to try to defend God do not work. Whatever misfortunes may befall us, we ought not to attempt to appease God by pleading guilty to false charges. Whenever we find injustice, we are to condemn it and speak up for those who suffer from it. When decent, law-abiding people are afflicted with sickness or misfortune, we should never tell them that they are only getting what they deserve. There is yet another lesson. When the Psalmist asks, "What is man that You are mindful of him?" (Ps. 8:5), the book of Job answers by showing us a man who even in the depths of agony can rise to heroic proportions. While such heroism does not provide a justification of innocent suffering, it does provide a model for how we should respond to it.

Conclusion

The Legacy of the Prophets

Having looked at the prophets over the course of eight chapters, I hope to leave you with three observations and one final point. The observations concern how much of the story of the prophets is truly astonishing—even miraculous. The final point has to do with what the prophets are trying to tell us about Judaism as a whole.

The Real Miracles

Throughout this book, I have avoided the question of whether prophetic experience is miraculous, a natural awakening of the human mind, or something else. There is no way to know which is right, and besides, the important point is not how we ourselves characterize the experience, but what messages such experiences are trying to convey. To me, what is miraculous is not that God singled out a certain people to act as messengers but that despite the controversial nature of their message, they continue to occupy such an essential part of the sacred literature of Judaism.

As we saw in chapter 3, First Isaiah followed Amos and Hosea in saying that God loathes the people's festivals and will not accept their sacrifices. In chapter 5, we read Jeremiah's prediction that God is about to abandon Jerusalem—and, further, that God is saying: "Shall I not bring retribution / On a nation such as this?" In chapter 6, we considered Ezekiel's claims: The Temple is full of detestable things; God will destroy Jerusalem and mock it among the other nations of the world. What other people has subjected itself to such scathing self-criticism and encouraged everyone else to read it?

It is clear, then, that much of prophetic literature is negative in tone and paints the Jewish people in an unfavorable light. As the biblical historian John Barton put it, such literature is subversive, undercutting the foundations of established religion.[1] While it does include messages of consolation, those messages come after strongly worded rebukes and warnings of impending disaster. For example, both Jeremiah's vision of a new covenant between God and Israel (Jer. 31:31–34) and Ezekiel's dry bones vision symbolizing a reborn Israel (Ezek. 37:1–6) appear after lengthy descriptions of divine anger and the suffering that will have to be endured before justice prevails. It is human nature to recoil at such criticism and pretend that things are not as bad as the prophets say. That is why it is nothing short of amazing that these writings were preserved rather than destroyed.

Scholars estimate that the writings of the prophets were finalized around 300 BCE, roughly 150 to 200 years after the age of prophecy came to a close. Although we will never know all the editorial decisions that were made when these writings became part of the biblical canon, we can say that in view of Israel's history, major changes took place. Our overview of that history showed that the Northern Kingdom was destroyed by the Assyrians in 722 BCE and the Southern Kingdom (including Jerusalem) by the Babylonians in 586 BCE. Although the Persians allowed the people exiled by the Babylonians to return to Jerusalem in 538 BCE, it was clear that Israel was now part of a large empire that had its own gods and its own religion. In 331 BCE, Alexander the Great overtook Persia and amassed an even larger empire. One explanation for all that befell Israel is that God became displeased with it and no longer felt duty bound to protect it. We therefore can understand why *some* criticism of Israel would make it into the biblical canon..

What seems miraculous is the extent and the graphic nature of the criticism. Was Israel really on a level with Sodom? Did God take pleasure in mocking it in front of the other nations? Not only was this literature preserved, but in a later age, the Rabbis decided that, with the exception of Job, it should be read on the Sabbath and festival days. In doing so, they ran the risk that the rebukes were so severe and the standards for success so high that people would become dispirited and abandon the whole tradition. Risky or not, the decision stood. The result is that, for us, part of worship consists in reviewing how Israel broke its promises, turned to other gods, abused the poor, and tried to appease God by sacrificing animals and singing hymns.

If it is miraculous that Judaism canonized self-criticism, it is equally miraculous that despite numerous massacres, expulsions, and persecutions, it still survives. As I see it, these miracles are related. In other words, one of the features that have kept the spirit of the Jewish People alive is its willingness to tolerate — even canonize — self-criticism. Rather than be satisfied with a steady diet of platitudes, Judaism opened its ranks to those who challenged conventional ways of thinking and forced people to reexamine their understanding of what religion is supposed to be. More than a formidable army or an impenetrable fortress, it is Judaism's willingness to hear dissenting voices that has distinguished it from the long list of peoples whose religions have vanished into obscurity.

Paramount among the questions the prophets raised is whether any religion can claim validity if it ignores the ethical import of its teachings. We saw in chapter 1 that according to Amos, religious practice is a sham if it does nothing to motivate better behavior. We saw in chapter 8 that God is not enamored of the kind of theodicy offered by Job's friends. These insights lead us to ask whether we can separate service to God from care for the poor or the sick.

What would it say about God if we could? Can we serve God in the conviction that doing so will guarantee health and prosperity? Again, what would it say about God if we could? These are only examples of the questions the prophets raised, but they show how far reaching the questions are.

Although they did not produce a systematic theology, the prophets did much to lay the groundwork on which such theologies were built. We have seen that thinkers as diverse as Maimonides, Kant, Cohen,

Buber, Levinas, and Soloveitchik constructed systems of thought that incorporated prophetic insights. This too is miraculous. Who would have thought that insights garnered from a breeder of cattle (Amos) would dovetail so nicely with the thought of Kant? Who would have thought that Second Isaiah would lay the groundwork for Maimonides and virtually all thinkers in the monotheistic tradition? By the same token, who would have thought the writings of a priest living in exile in Babylonia (Ezekiel) would have a dramatic impact on Cohen and Soloveitchik? The answer is that no one would have thought it, which makes this aspect of the prophetic legacy as astonishing as the other two.

The Final Point

What, then, are the prophets trying to tell us? In one way or another, all the people we have studied have called into question the idea that Judaism consists exclusively of rituals or ceremonies to be performed at special times or in special places. As they saw it, Judaism is a full-time endeavor dealing with every aspect of life: from compassion for the poor to honesty in the marketplace, from justice in the courts to the need to work for peace, from hope in the future to the ability to take responsibility for one's actions, from the courage to suffer for a righteous cause to the good sense not to trust in idols, omens, or good-luck charms.

Thus the message of the prophets is that nothing is completely secular. No sphere of life is absent of religious or spiritual significance. Every contact with another person, every assessment of one's own actions or attitudes, every plan or purpose has a spiritual dimension to it. It is not that God will bring down whole cities if we forget this but that as children of prophets, we are called upon to carry their message forward. So even if their contemporaries ignored their messages, we would do well to take them to heart.

Notes

Preface

1. Brettler, *How to Read the Jewish Bible*, 138.
2. In view of this approach, questions of what the prophets actually said and what was added by later editors or redactors—issues discussed at length by other authors—do not appear in this volume.
3. A character named Job is mentioned at Gen. 46:13, but is it unclear whether he is the same person as the title character of the book of Job.

Introduction

1. According to a parenthetical remark at 1 Sam. 9:9, *navi* came to replace *roeh* (seer). In other words, if a person wanted to know God's will, she or he would approach a seer and then, according to changed usage, a prophet.
2. Kugel, *The Great Shift*, 108.
3. Heschel, *The Prophets*, 1:x.
4. The Hebrew word translated as "young woman" is *almah*, which means that the woman is of marriageable age. However, the Greek translation rendered *almah* as *parthenos*, which means "a virgin." In the Christian reading, then, Isaiah is predicting that a virgin will give birth to a son.
5. Maimonides, *Guide of the Perplexed* 2.32, 2.36. For an excellent survey of medieval attempts to explain biblical prophecy, see Kriesel, *Prophecy: The History of an Idea in Medieval Jewish Philosophy*.
6. Schwartz, *Path of the Prophets*, xviii–xix.
7. For a prophet who took money, see 1 Sam. 9:7. But see also Mic. 3:11, which recounts God's anger at prophets who take money.
8. See 1 Sam. 9:20; 2 Kings 2:3, 2:5, 2:7, 4:1, 4:38, 5:22, and 6:1.

9. See also 2 Kings 3:15–16, where Elisha asks for a musician when asked to prophesize.
10. See Harissis, "A Bittersweet Story."
11. Friedman, *The Hidden Face of God*, 22, 63–65.
12. See Maimonides, *Mishneh Torah* 1, Basic Principles, 9.1, where, speaking of prophets, Maimonides says "whether Jewish or gentile."
13. Halevi, *Kuzari*, 1.95, 1.99, 1.115, 2.10–14, 3.1, 4.10.
14. The reason for thinking that First Isaiah came from a priestly family is that his call (6:1–8) seems to have taken place in a part of the Temple to which only priests were admitted. For a moving account of this experience, see Buber, *The Prophetic Faith*, 158–59.
15. Walzer, *In God's Shadow*, 75–76.
16. According to Walzer, Elijah was the only prophet who got to name a successor.
17. See Buber, *The Prophetic Faith*, 128: "Hardly ever does he [the prophet] foretell a plainly certain future. YHVH does not deliver into his hand a completed book of fate with all future events written in it, calling upon him to open it in the presence of the hearers."
18. Heschel, *The Prophets*, 1:12.
19. Kugel, *The Great Shift*, 240 and following.
20. Kaufmann, *The Religion of Ancient Israel*, 353.
21. Jer. 23:14 says that God is so incensed with the false prophets of Jerusalem that he considers them worse than the people of Sodom and Gomorrah.
22. By contrast, Ps. 46 and 48 suggest that Jerusalem will never be destroyed.
23. There is a vigorous scholarly debate on whether this assessment is true. For a well-argued defense of the traditional position and review of the scholarly literature that questions it, see Sommer, "Did Prophecy Cease? Evaluating a Reevaluation." For a recent discussion of the conflicting views of ancient sources on the end of prophecy, see Kugel, *The Great Shift*, 230–55.
24. See Deut. 31:16–21 and 2 Kings 17:7–8, which say essentially the same thing.
25. Heschel, *Prophetic Inspiration after the Prophets*.
26. See *Guide of the Perplexed* 2, Introduction, 3.51, as well as *Mishneh Torah* 1, Basic Principles, 9.1.
27. The renowned biblical scholar Julius Wellhausen argued that contrary to what we might think, the direction of influence did not go from the Torah to the prophets but the other way around. In other words, much of the prophetic works were written down before the Torah was completed. If this is true, it is unclear how much of the Torah the prophets knew. See

Wellhausen, *Prolegomena to the History of Israel*. For a modern discussion, see Brettler, *How to Read the Jewish Bible*, 150–51.

28. Friedman, *The Hidden Face of God*.
29. A likely explanation is offered by Kugel, *The Great Shift*, 235, who suggests that prophecy did not so much cease as transform itself.
30. Buber, *The Prophetic Faith*, 211.
31. Buber, *The Prophetic Faith*, 57.
32. Buber, *The Prophetic Faith*, 3.
33. Buber, *The Prophetic Faith*, 213.
34. Buber, *The Prophetic Faith*, 213.

1. Amos

1. To this day, scholars debate how much of what is collected in the book of Amos consists of words that Amos actually spoke some 2,500 years ago and how much consists of later additions. Throughout the ancient world, students or disciples commonly wrote in the name of their teacher rather than their own name in order to preserve the spirit of their teacher's message.
2. Compare with Deut. 16:20: "Justice, justice shall you pursue, that you may thrive and occupy the land that the LORD your God is giving you."
3. Buber, *The Prophetic Faith*, 121.
4. Maimonides, *Guide of the Perplexed*, 525–31.
5. See, for example, Gen. 18:19: "For I have singled him [Abraham] out, that he may instruct his children and his posterity to keep the way of the LORD by doing what is just and right." Also see Deut. 8:6, Ps. 119:3, Ps. 128:1, Mic. 4:2, Zech. 19:9.
6. On this issue, see Lev. 9–11, where Aaron's sons Nadav and Avihu are killed for not following the proper rules.
7. A variety of considerations, in particular the reference to the royal line of David at 9:11, suggest that this passage is a later addition. For further discussion, see Brettler, *How to Read the Jewish Bible*, 159–60.
8. Kaufmann, *The Religion of Ancient Israel*, 402.
9. Heschel, *The Prophets*, 1:14.
10. Heschel, *The Prophets*, 1:15.
11. Maimonides, *Guide of the Perplexed*, 525–31. It should be noted, however, that according to Maimonides, the commandments regarding sacrifices represented God's concession to human fallibility. Because the people were accustomed to seeing animals be sacrificed, God had no choice but to include such commandments in Mosaic legislation.

12. *Berachot* 45a, *Eruvin* 14b. Note, as Sommer, *Revelation and Authority*, 126, does, that in this context "people" does not mean *any* people but those who observe the law.

13. *Bava Batra* 60b, *Bava Kamma* 70b, *Avodah Zarah* 36a, *Horayot* 3b. Also see *Beitzah* 30a, where the Rabbis decide to "let Israel be."

14. Aristotle, *Nicomachean Ethics* 1099a31–1099b8.

15. Hegel, *Philosophy of Right*, 10.

16. For Hegel's mixed reaction to the Prussia of his day, see Taylor, *Hegel*, 425–26, 452–61.

17. Hegel, *Philosophy of Right*, 213–14.

18. Plato, *Gorgias* 481b–c.

19. Kant, *Critique of Practical Reason*, 123.

20. Kant, *Critique of Pure Reason*, A313/B370.

21. Heschel, *The Prophets*, 1:165. Compare with Kant, *Religion within the Boundaries of Mere Reason*, 6:19–20.

22. Heschel, *The Prophets*, 1:15.

23. Compare Deut. 4:5–8, where Moses says that Israel will be an example to all the other nations. Also see Isa. 42:6, where Israel is to serve as a "light unto the nations." Although some have questioned whether the latter passage refers to a single individual or the nation as a whole, a reasonable understanding is that it refers to the nation.

24. Kaufmann, *The Religion of Ancient Israel*, 420.

25. See Walzer, *In God's Shadow*, 88: "No prophet . . . showed any interest in politics of reform or any readiness for the compromises this might require."

2. Hosea

1. For an excellent account of the development of the concept of idolatry, see Halbertal and Margalit, *Idolatry*.

2. See Deut. 31:16–17; the whoring metaphor occurs near the end of the Torah.

3. Kaufmann, *The Religion of Ancient Israel*, 142–43.

4. Maimonides, *Guide of the Perplexed*, 387, 406.

5. According to 1 Kings 21:1–4 and 2 Kings 9: 21–35, the Jezreel Valley was the sight of a bloody massacre where King Jehu (842–15 BCE) defeated the followers of Ahab and Jezebel. Yet Hosea thinks that God is angry at Jehu. Thus Hosea 1:3–4: "Name him Jezreel; for I will soon punish the House of Jehu [presumably Israel] for the bloody deeds at Jezreel and put an end to the monarchy of the House of Israel. In that day, I will break the bow of Israel in the Valley of Jezreel."

6. The cult of Baal, a deity thought to be responsible for fertility, may have involved prostitutes and ritual intercourse.

7. Admah and Zeboiim are cities destroyed along with Sodom and Gomorrah.

8. Heschel, *The Prophets*, 1:26. For an extended critique of Heschel based on the idea that he has succumbed to literal interpretation of biblical language, see Berkovits, "Dr. A. J. Heschel's Theology of Pathos."

9. Heschel, *The Prophets*, 2:4.

10. For a brief history of "pathos" and "pathetic," see Heschel, *The Prophets*, 2:269–72.

11. Maimonides, *Guide of the Perplexed*, 126–27.

12. Maimonides, *Guide of the Perplexed*, 81.

13. Maimonides, *Guide of the Perplexed*, 82. Emphasis in original.

14. For more on the topic of how to read the Bible, see Seeskin, *Thinking about the Torah*, 1–13.

15. An accessible English translation of Maimonides, "Helek Sanhedrin, Chapter Ten," can be found in Maimonides, *A Maimonides Reader*, 401–23.

16. Maimonides, *Guide of the Perplexed*, 123–25.

17. Exod. 34:7 says that God will visit the sins of the parents on the children and the children's children to the third and fourth generations. But see Ezek. 18:1–3 for a different view.

18. Heschel, *The Prophets*, 2:5.

19. A possible counterexample can be found at Isa. 54:7–8, which says that God's anger burned *for a moment*. But it also says that God will take Israel back in kindness and love, so it is not necessarily a counterexample to the argument.

3. First Isaiah, Part 1

1. Some scholars argue that even chapters 1–39 (First Isaiah) contain the writings of multiple authors.

2. See McNeill, "The Plague That Saved Jerusalem, 701 B.C."

3. Although these figures are probably exaggerated, the war, especially as it was a war of two against one, would have brought significant death and destruction. See also 2 Kings 16:5–6.

4. Buber, *The Prophetic Faith*, 167.

5. Thucydides, *The Peloponnesian War*, 330–37.

6. Buber, *The Prophetic Faith*, 167.

7. Walzer, *In God's Shadow*, 103–4.

8. Heschel, *The Prophets*, 1:82.

9. For further discussion of this passage and its implications, see Seeskin, *Thinking about the Torah*, 101–12.

10. Levinas, *Difficult Freedom*, 199.

4. First Isaiah, Part 2

1. Also see Isa. 9:2–7 and Jer. 23:5.

2. Maimonides, *Mishneh Torah* 14, Kings and Wars, 11.1.

3. This is an adaptation and not the exact wording of Maimonides' twelfth principle.

4. Scholem, *The Messianic Idea in Judaism*, 35.

5. Josephus, *The Jewish War*, 6.312–13. As Josephus goes on to say, the oracle was actually about the Roman emperor Vespasian.

6. Graetz, "The Stages in the Evolution of the Messianic Belief," 151–52.

7. See, for example, Mishnah *Berachot* 1:5.

8. Neusner, "Messianic Themes in Formative Judaism," 357–74. For further discussion of the philosophic implications of Rabbinic conceptions of the Messiah, see Seeskin, *Jewish Messianic Thoughts in an Age of Despair*, 17–19.

9. The origin of this tradition is unclear, but see Klausner, *The Messianic Idea in Israel*, 400–401, 520–21. For a Rabbinic precedent, see *Sukkah* 52a. For a modern discussion, see Liver, "The Doctrine of the Two Messiahs," 149–85. Some speculate that this doctrine is analogous to the Second Coming of Jesus.

10. Neusner, "Messianic Themes in Formative Judaism," 357.

11. Maimonides, *Mishneh Torah* 14, Kings and Wars, 11.3, 12.1. For Rabbinic sources, see *Berachot* 34b, *Shabbat* 63a, 151b, *Sanhedrin* 91b and 99a. Maimonides presents a more traditional view of the Messiah in his "Epistle to Yemen," a letter written to a Jewish community in distress in which he claims there will be cosmic upheavals and the Messiah will work wonders. But as Hartman, *Crisis and Leadership: Epistles of Maimonides*, 172, astutely observes: "The *Epistle to Yemen* cannot be treated as a paradigm of Maimonides' theory of messianism or history."

12. Maimonides, *Mishneh Torah* 14, Kings and Wars, 11.3. As many people have noted, this raises a question about resurrection, which not only is a miracle but in Maimonides' opinion a fundamental principle of Jewish belief. For a translation and insightful commentary on Maimonides' treatise on resurrection, see Hartman, *Crisis and Leadership*, 209–80.

13. Maimonides, *A Maimonides Reader*, 414–16. Note that when Isaiah says that the promised king will judge the poor with equity (11:1), this implies that there will still be poor people during his reign.

14. Maimonides, *Mishneh Torah* 14, Kings and Wars, 12.5.

15. Kellner, *Science in the Bet Midrash*, 291; and Kellner, "Messianic Postures in Israel Today," 504–9.

16. Maimonides, *Mishneh Torah* 14, Kings and Wars, 11.4.

17. This text, which was once censored, comes from the end of Maimonides, *Mishneh Torah* 14, Kings and Wars, 11.

18. Cohen, *Religion of Reason*, 261.

19. Cohen, *Religion of Reason*, 248, 262, 289–91.

20. Cohen, *Reason and Hope*, 127.

21. Cohen, *Reason and Hope*, 123–24.

22. Cohen, *Religion of Reason*, 207.

23. Cohen, *Religion of Reason*, 314–15.

24. Schwarzschild, *The Pursuit of the Ideal*, 211. See also Patterson, "Though the Messiah May Tarry," 16: "The Messiah is by definition *the one who tarries*, signifying a redemption that is *always yet to be*, always future, because what we do now is never *enough*."

25. Schwarzschild made this criticism at an early stage in his career. See Schwarzschild, *Pursuit of the Ideal*, 19.

26. Rosenzweig, *Briefe und Tagebucher*, 2:1150.

27. Moltmann, *The Experiment Hope*, 89. In this passage, Moltmann reflects on the thought of Dostoevsky.

5. Jeremiah

1. See Deut. 30:14. When God's word is in people's hearts, then presumably there will be no need for the Ark of the Covenant (Jer. 3:16).

2. Other reluctant leaders include Saul (1 Sam. 9) and Gideon (Judg. 6).

3. Plato, *The Republic* 520d.

4. Heschel, *The Prophets*, 1:121.

5. Buber, *The Prophetic Faith*, 204.

6. Buber, *The Prophetic Faith*, 203. Note Buber's next sentence: "The contact between godhead and manhood in his [Jeremiah's] view is not bound up with the rite but with the *word*."

7. See, for example, Blenkinsopp, *A History of Prophecy in Israel*, 146–47.

8. Kant, *Religion within the Boundaries of Mere Reason*, 6:36–37. Note that both Jeremiah (17:9) and Kant seem to regard the evil dictates of the heart as inscrutable.

9. Equally controversial is the passage's assertion of the doctrine of vicarious atonement: the belief that *A*'s suffering can atone for *B*'s sins.

10. Russell, "A Free Man's Worship," 113.

11. Kant, *The Metaphysics of Morals*, 250–51.

12. Cohen, *Religion of Reason*, 136.

13. Cohen, *Religion of Reason*, 142.

14. Cohen, *Religion of Reason*, 16–17.

15. Buber, *The Prophetic Faith*, 225.

16. The text references the traditional rendering of this passage rather than the current NJPS translation, which reads: "For I desire goodness, not sacrifice; / Obedience to God, rather than burnt offerings."

6. Ezekiel

1. See *Shabbat* 13b.

2. For further discussion, see Brettler, *How to Read the Jewish Bible*, 185–86. Note, as Brettler does, that the *Mekhilta de-Rabbi Ishmael* says explicitly that after the Land of Israel had been chosen, all other lands were eliminated as sites for divine revelation.

3. For criticism of this view, see Leibowitz, *Judaism, Human Values, and the Jewish State*, 86–87.

4. Halevi, *Kuzari*, 2.9–24.

5. Buber, *The Prophetic Faith*, 209–10. Buber also objects that centralized worship compromises much of the continuity and naturalness of the religious life of the people. See also Sommer, *Revelation and Authority*, 72: "On a practical level, by commanding the centralization of the sacrificial cult in a single Temple, D [Deuteronomy] removes the Temple from the religious lives of most Israelites, and therefore it must provide other rituals to take the place of the local temple or altar."

6. See, for example, Jer. 18:7–8.

7. Ezek. 22:2, 24:6. In addition to being gruesome, this terminology may well indicate that Jerusalem is impure.

8. See Ezek. 5:11, 7:4, and 9:5–6.

9. As Blenkinsopp, *A History of Prophecy in Israel*, 175, notes, the idea that Israel is and always will be undeserving of God's grace has been seen as a forerunner to the Protestant doctrine of *sola gratia*, that redemption comes solely from the grace of God rather than from anything humans have done to merit it.

10. For an attempt to psychoanalyze Ezekiel on the basis of these and similar passages, see Halperin, *Seeking Ezekiel*.

11. Also see 8:1–4 and 40:1–3.

12. For more on this topic, see Scholem, *Jewish Gnosticism, Merkabah Mysticism, and Talmudic Tradition*.

13. Maimonides, *Guide of the Perplexed*, 6–7.

14. Maimonides, *Guide of the Perplexed*, 417–30. This picture presupposes a geocentric view of the universe, according to which the stars and planets are embedded in concentric spheres whose point of rotation is the center of the earth.
15. For a defense of the flawed science view, see Davies, *Method and Metaphysics in Maimonides' Guide of the Perplexed*, 106–60.
16. Cohen, *Religion of Reason*, 177.
17. The morality of such examples is questioned by Sommer in *Revelation and Authority*, 27.
18. See, however, Deut. 24:16, which says that parents should not be put to death for the sins of their children nor children for the sins of their parents.
19. A similar sentiment is expressed at Ezek. 14:12 and following.
20. Maimonides, *Guide of the Perplexed*, 436–37.
21. The same sentiment was expressed by Pope Benedict XVI, as quoted in Sommer, *Revelation and Authority*, 97: "It is necessary to keep in mind that any human utterance of a certain weight contains more than the author may have been immediately aware of at the time."
22. Kant, *Religion within the Boundaries of Mere Reason* , 6:44. As for how Kant, a Christian, perceived the doctrine of original sin, he viewed Adam and Eve's action as symbolic of the human condition. Rather than passing on their guilt to others, Adam and Eve offered the paradigm of what sin is like: rebellion against the decrees of God. When we sin, it is as if we have reenacted their transgression.
23. On this issue, see Cohen's treatment of the evil impulse (*yetzer ha-ra*) in Cohen, *Religion of Reason*, 181–82.
24. Cohen, *Religion of Reason*, 186.
25. Cohen, *Religion of Reason*, 195.
26. Maimonides, *Mishneh Torah*, Laws of Repentance, 5.1–2.
27. Cohen, *Religion of Reason*, 193.
28. *Ethics of the Fathers* 2.14.
29. *Ethics of the Fathers* 4.22.
30. Cohen, *Religion of Reason*, 202–3.
31. Cohen, *Religion of Reason*, 201.
32. Cohen, *Religion of Reason*, 209.
33. Cohen, *Religion of Reason*, 209.
34. Soloveitchik, *Halakhic Man*, 110–17. For an insightful comparison between Cohen and Soloveitchik, see Kaplan, "Hermann Cohen and Rabbi Joseph Soloveitchik on Repentance," 213–58.
35. Soloveitchik, *Halakhic Man*, 113.

36. Soloveitchik, *Halakhic Man*, 115.

37. Soloveitchik, *Halakhic Man*, 117.

38. Soloveitchik, *Halakhic Man*, 117.

7. Second Isaiah

1. The legend that Abraham smashed his father's idols comes from a midrash. See *Genesis Rabbah* 38:13.

2. Note that the *Mi Chamocha* prayer is taken from this passage. Emphasis mine.

3. Also see 43:10–13 and 45: 6–7. A similar claim is made at Deut. 4:35, which may have been contemporaneous with Second Isaiah.

4. Cohen, *Religion of Reason*, 35.

5. Brettler, *How to Read the Jewish Bible*, 202–3.

6. Maimonides, *Guide of the Perplexed* 2.12, see also 3.51.

7. Maimonides, *Guide of the Perplexed* 1.57.

8. Kugel, *The God of Old*, 36 and following.

9. According to Hosea 12, Jacob confronted God at Peniel.

10. Kugel, *The God of Old*, 61.

11. Seeskin, *Thinking about the Torah*, 102–3.

12. *Exodus Rabbah* 34:1; *Numbers Rabbah* 11:5.

13. *Megillah* 29a; *Sotah* 5a; *Sanhedrin* 46a.

14. The precise nature of the *Shekhinah* has long been a subject of debate. Joshua Abelson, *The Immanence of God in Rabbinic Literature*, argues that it is an incarnation of God. For those who think the Bible is committed to the idea of a hypostasis, or separate entity, see Friedman, *The Hidden Face of God*, 13; and Sommer, *The Bodies of God and the World of Ancient Israel*, 59. By contrast, Ephraim Urbach, *The Sages*, 634, argues that the *Shekhinah* is neither an incarnation nor a separate entity.

15. Heschel, *Between God and Man*, 102.

16. Josephus, *The Jewish War* 6.288 and following.

17. Gersonides, *Wars of the Lord*, 2:33–37; 3:56–78.

18. See, for example, *King Lear* 1.1, 109–12; 1.2, 103–37. But see as well *Julius Caesar* 1.2.17.

19. For Maimonides' Letter on Astrology, see Lerner, *Maimonides' Empire of Light*, 178–87. Also see Maimonides, *Guide of the Perplexed* 3.37.

20. See *Sanhedrin* 39b, *Genesis Rabbah* 8:4, and Rashi's commentary on Gen. 21:17.

21. For the night prayer, see Birnbaum, *Daily Prayer Book*, 784.

22. Schechter, *Aspects of Rabbinic Theology*, 291–92. See also Cohen, *Religion of Reason*, 48, who says that divine uniqueness excludes any mediation between God and natural existence.

23. Levinas, *Difficult Freedom*, 14. For Maimonides' attempt to de-charm the medieval world, see Kellner, *Maimonides' Confrontation with Mysticism*.

24. Here, the present author follows in the footsteps of Louis Jacobs, *A Jewish Theology*, 290–91.

25. By contrast, Maimonides' understanding of idolatry was severe. According to him, anyone who believes that God has multiple attributes, say wisdom and goodness, or is material or experiences emotion, is an idolater. By personal estimation, this would include more than 90 percent of the Jews who have ever lived, including many prominent rabbis and theologians.

26. Heschel, *God in Search of Man*, 142.

8. Job

1. It is worth mentioning that the Satan who appears in this story is not yet the daemonic figure known to Christianity or Milton's *Paradise Lost*. His skepticism regarding Job is perfectly justified. How can we assess Job's faithfulness unless he is tested?

2. Maimonides, *Guide of the Perplexed* 2.23, thought that the true meaning of the book of Job could be found in Elihu's speech and God's speech from the whirlwind, both of which stress the limits of human understanding.

3. For further discussion, see Larrimore, *The Book of Job: A Biography*, 218.

4. The Greek translation, or Septuagint, is shorter than the Hebrew original, and even when the missing lines are accounted for, the translation is not always accurate. Compare the two at 3:20, 9:13, 9:22, 12:6, 14:16, 16:13–14, 19:6, and 23:7. For further discussion of this problem, see Geman, "The Theological Approach of the Greek Translator of Job 1–15," 231–40; Gard, "The Concept of Job's Character According to the Greek Translation of the Hebrew Text," 182–86; Orlinsky, "Studies in the Septuagint of the Book of Job."

5. Pope, *The Anchor Bible: Job*, xv.

6. The issue concerns how to translate the Hebrew *lo ayahel*. The basis of the "Yet will I trust in Him" reading is a marginal note in the manuscript. But the context is more consistent with rebellion than perseverance.

7. For a brief discussion of the alternatives, see Brettler, *How to Read the Jewish Bible*, 253–54.

8. *Sotah* 31a, *Bava Batra* 16a.

9. *Sotah* 31a. Note, however, that this interpretation is based on the reading of 13:15 in which Job is patient and persistent.

10. *Bava Batra* 16a.

11. See Larrimore, *The Book of Job: A Biography*, 15: "There are registers of religious expression — such as lament and protest — that saccharine modern understandings of religion can no longer imagine."

12. *Berachot* 32a. For further discussion of this theme, see Blank, "Men against God: The Promethean Element in Biblical Prayer," 1–13.

13. See also Ps. 13:2, 44:24–27.

14. Levenson, *Creation and the Persistence of Evil*, xvii. Although I agree with Levenson on this point, I am not convinced that Job ends his quest with unqualified submission to God (xviii).

15. Kant, "On the Miscarriage of All Philosophical Trials in Theodicy," 27.

16. A *goel* is an advocate, avenger, or redeemer (usually a kinsman) who seeks to redress a wrong or correct a loss. The fact that Job says his *goel* will stand on earth does not show that he is thinking of someone other than God. Numerous biblical passages refer to God as a *goel*, for example, Exod. 6:6, 15:13; Isa. 41:14, 43:14, 44:6, 47:4. The idea here is that God will correct the wrong to which Job is now subject.

17. Gordis, *The Book of God and Man*, 119.

18. Maimonides, *Guide of the Perplexed* 3.22–23.

19. Kant, "On the Miscarriage of All Philosophical Trials in Theodicy," 32–33.

20. Kant, "On the Miscarriage of All Philosophical Trials in Theodicy," 33.

Conclusion

1. John Barton, *A History of the Bible*, 111.

Bibliography

Abelson, Joshua. *The Immanence of God in Rabbinic Literature*. London: Macmillan, 1912.

Barton, John. *A History of the Bible*. New York: Viking, 2019.

Berkovitz, Eliezer, "Dr. A. J. Heschel's Theology of Pathos." *Tradition: A Journal of Orthodox Jewish Thought* 6, no. 2 (1964): 67–104.

Berlin, Adele, and Marc Zvi Brettler, eds. *The Jewish Study Bible*. 2nd ed. New York: Oxford University Press, 2004.

Birnbaum, Philip. *Daily Prayer Book*. New York: Hebrew Publishing Company, 1977.

Blank, Sheldon H. "Men against God: The Promethean Element in Biblical Prayer." *Journal of Biblical Literature* 72 (1953): 1–13.

Blenkinsopp, Joseph. *A History of Prophecy in Israel*. Louisville KY: Westminster John Knox Press, 1996.

Brettler, Marc Zvi. *How to Read the Jewish Bible*. New York: Oxford University Press, 2007.

Buber, Martin. *The Prophetic Faith*. Princeton NJ: Princeton University Press, 2016.

Cohen, Hermann. *Reason and Hope*. Edited and translated by Eva Jospe. New York: W. W. Norton, 1971.

———. *Religion of Reason out of the Sources of Judaism*. Translated by Simon Kaplan. Atlanta GA: Scholars Press, 1995.

Davies, Daniel. *Method and Metaphysics in Maimonides' Guide of the Perplexed*. Oxford: Oxford University Press, 201

Friedman, Richard Elliott. *Commentary on the Torah*. New York: HarperCollins, 2001.

———. *The Hidden Face of God*. New York: HarperCollins, 1995.

———. *Who Wrote the Bible?* New York: HarperCollins, 1987.

Eskenazi, Tamara Cohen, and Andrea L. Weiss. *The Torah: A Woman's Commentary*. New York: URJ Press, 2007.

Gard, D. H. "The Concept of Job's Character According to the Greek Translation of the Hebrew Text." *Journal of Biblical Literature* 72 (1953): 182–86.

Geman, H. S. "The Theological Approach of the Greek Translator of Job 1–15." *Journal of Biblical Literature* 68 (1949): 231–40.

Gersonides. *The Wars of the Lord*. Vols. 2 and 3 Translated by Seymour Feldman. Philadelphia: The Jewish Publication Society, 1987 and 1999.

Gordis, Robert. *The Book of God and Man*. Chicago: University of Chicago Press, 1965.

Graetz, Heinrich. "The Stages in the Evolution of the Messianic Belief." In *The Structure of Jewish History and Other Essays*. Translated by Ismar Schorsch. New York: Jewish Theological Seminary, 1975.

Halbertal, Moshe, and Avishai Margalit. *Idolatry*. Translated by Naomi Goldblum. Cambridge MA: Harvard University Press, 1992.

Halevi, Judah. *Kuzari*. Translated by Chanan Morrison. CreateSpace Independent Publishing Platform, 2017.

Halperin, David J. *Seeking Ezekiel*. University Park: Pennsylvania State University, 1993.

Harissis, Haralampos V. "A Bittersweet Story: The True Nature of the Laurel of the Oracle of Delphi." *Perspectives in Biology and Medicine* 57:3 (Summer 2014): 351–60.

Hartman, David. *Crisis and Leadership: Epistles of Maimonides*. Philadelphia: The Jewish Publication Society, 1985.

Hegel. *Philosophy of Right*. Translated by T. M. Knox. Oxford: Oxford University Press, 1952.

Held, Shai. *Abraham Joshua Heschel: The Call of Transcendence*. Bloomington: Indiana University Press, 2013.

Heschel, Abraham Joshua. *Between God and Man*. New York: Free Press, 1959.

———. *God in Search of Man: A Philosophy of Judaism*. New York: Farrar, Straus and Giroux, 1983.

———. *Prophetic Inspiration after the Prophets: Maimonides and Other Medieval Authorities*. Hoboken: KTAV Publishing, 1996.

———. *The Prophets*. 2 vols. New York: Harper & Row, 1969.

Hick, John. *Evil and the God of Love*. London: Macmillan, 1966.

Jacobs, Louis. *A Jewish Theology*. New York: Behrman House, 1973.

Josephus. *Jewish Antiquities*. Books 1–3. Translated by H. St. J. Thackeray. Cambridge MA: Harvard University Press, 1930.

Kant, Immanuel. *Critique of Practical Reason*. Translated by Mary Gregor. Cambridge: Cambridge University Press, 1997.

———. *Critique of Pure Reason*. Translated by Paul Guyer and Allen W. Wood. Cambridge: Cambridge University Press, 1998.

———. *The Metaphysics of Morals*. Translated by Mary Gregor. Cambridge: Cambridge University Press, 1991.

———. "On the Miscarriage of All Philosophical Trials in Theodicy." In *Religion and Rational Theology*. Translated by A. Wood and G. Giovanni. Cambridge: Cambridge University Press, 1996.

———. *Religion within the Boundaries of Mere Reason*. Translated by A. Wood and G. Di Giovanni. Cambridge: Cambridge University Press, 1998.

Kaplan, Lawrence. "Hermann Cohen and Rabbi Joseph Soloveitchik on Repentance." *Journal of Jewish Thought and Philosophy* 13:1–2 (2004): 213–58.

Kaufmann, Yehezkel. *The Religion of Ancient Israel*. Translated by Moshe Greenberg. New York: Schocken Books, 1972.

Kellner, Menachem. *Maimonides' Confrontation with Mysticism*. Oxford: Littman Library of Jewish Civilization, 2006.

———. "Messianic Postures in Israel Today." In *Essential Papers on Messianic Movements and Personalities in Jewish History*. Edited by Marc Saperstein. New York: NYU Press, 1992.

———. *Science in the Bet Midrash*. Brighton MA: Academic Studies Press, 2009.

Klausner, Joseph. *The Messianic Idea in Israel*. Translated by W. F. Stinespring. New York: Macmillan, 1955.

Kriesel, Howard. *Prophecy: The History of an Idea in Medieval Jewish Philosophy*. Dordrecht: Kluwer, 2001.

Kugel, James L. *The God of Old*. New York: Free Press, 2003.

———. *The Great Shift: Encountering God in Biblical Times*. Boston: Houghton Mifflin Harcourt, 2017.

———. *How to Read the Bible*. New York: Free Press, 2007.

Larrimore, Mark. *The Book of Job: A Biography*. Princeton NJ: Princeton University Press, 2013.

Leibowitz, Yeshayahu. *Judaism, Human Values, and the Jewish State*. Translated by Eliezer Goldman. Cambridge MA: Harvard University Press, 1992.

Lerner, Ralph. *Maimonides' Empire of Light*. Chicago: University of Chicago Press, 2000.

Levenson, Jon D. *Creation and the Persistence of Evil: The Jewish Drama of Divine Omnipotence*. Princeton NJ: Princeton University Press, 1994.

Levinas, Emmanuel. *Basic Philosophical Writings*. Edited by Adriaan T. Peperzak et al. Bloomington: Indiana University Press, 1996.

————. *Difficult Freedom: Essays on Judaism*. Translated by Sean Hand. Baltimore MD: Johns Hopkins University Press, 1990.

————. *The Levinas Reader*. Edited by Sean Hand. Oxford: Basil Blackwell, 1989.

Liver, J. J. "The Doctrine of the Two Messiahs." *Harvard Theological Review* 52 (1959): 149–85.

Maimonides, Moses. *Guide of the Perplexed*. Translated by Shlomo Pines. Chicago: University of Chicago Press, 1963.

————. *A Maimonides Reader*. Edited by Isadore Twersky. West Orange NJ: Behrman House, 1972.

————. *Mishneh Torah* (Code of Jewish Law). [In Hebrew.] Edited by S. T. Rubenstein et. al. Jerusalem: Mossad Harav Kook, 1967–73.

————. *Mishneh Torah*. Translated by E. Touger. New York: Moznaim Publishing, 1989.

McNeill, William, H. "The Plague That Saved Jerusalem, 701 B.C." In *What If?* Edited by Robert Cowley. New York: Berkeley Books, 1999.

Moltmann, Jurgen. *The Experiment Hope*. Translated by M. Douglas Meeks. Philadelphia: Fortress Press, 1975.

Morgan, Michael. *A Holocaust Reader*. Oxford: Oxford University Press, 2001.

Neusner, Jacob. "Messianic Themes in Formative Judaism." *Journal of the American Academy of Religion* 52 (1984): 357–74.

Newsome, James D., Jr. *The Hebrew Prophets*. Atlanta GA: John Knox Press, 1984.

Orlinsky, Harry. "Studies in the Septuagint of the Book of Job." *Hebrew Union College Annual* 28 (1957): 53–74, as well as 29 (1958): 229–71 and 30 (1959): 153–67.

Patterson, David. "Though the Messiah May Tarry." May Smith Lecture on Post-Holocaust Christian Jewish Dialogue, Florida Atlantic University, January 26, 2009.

Plaut, W. Gunther. *The Torah: A Modern Commentary*. New York: Union of American Hebrew Congregations, 1981.

Pope, Marvin. H. *The Anchor Bible: Job*. New Haven CT: Yale University Press, 1965.

Rosenzweig, Franz. *Briefe und Tagebucher*. Vol. 2. The Hague: Martinus Nijhoff, 1979.

————. *The Star of Redemption*. Translated by William W. Hallo. Notre Dame IN: University of Notre Dame Press, 1970.

Russell, Bertrand. "A Free Man's Worship." In *Why I Am Not a Christian*. New York: Harper & Row, 1963.

Sarna, Nahum M., ed. *The JPS Torah Commentary*, Genesis and Exodus. Philadelphia: The Jewish Publication Society, 1989 and 1991.

Sawyer, John F. A. *Prophecy and the Biblical Prophets*. Rev. ed. Oxford: Oxford University Press, 1989 and 1991.

Schechter, Solomon. *Aspects of Rabbinic Theology*. New York: Schocken Books, 1961.

Scholem, Gershom. *Jewish Gnosticism, Merkabah Mysticism, and Talmudic Tradition*. New York: Jewish Theological Seminary of America, 1960.

———. *The Messianic Idea in Judaism*. New York: Schocken Books, 1971.

Schwartz, Barry. *Path of the Prophets*. Philadelphia: The Jewish Publication Society, 2018.

Schwarzschild, Steven. *The Pursuit of the Ideal*. Edited by Menachem Kellner. Albany: SUNY Press, 1990.

Seeskin, Kenneth. *Jewish Messianic Thoughts in an Age of Despair*. New York: Cambridge University Press, 2012.

———. *Thinking about the Torah: A Philosopher Reads the Bible*. Philadelphia: The Jewish Publication Society, 2016.

Soloveitchik, Joseph B. *Halakhic Man*. Translated by Lawrence Kaplan. Philadelphia: The Jewish Publication Society, 1983.

Sommer, Benjamin D. *The Bodies of God and the World of Ancient Israel*. Cambridge: Cambridge University Press, 2009.

———. "Did Prophecy Cease?" *Journal of Biblical Literature* 115 (1996): 31–47.

———. *Revelation and Authority: Sinai in Jewish Scripture and Tradition*. New Haven CT: Yale University Press, 2015.

Taylor, Charles. *Hegel*. Cambridge: Cambridge University Press, 1975.

Thucydides. *The Peloponnesian War*. Translated by Richard Crawley. New York: Random House, 1951.

Urbach, Ephraim. *The Sages*. Translated by Israel Abrams. Jerusalem: Hebrew University Press, 1979.

Walzer, Michael. *Exodus and Revolution*. New York: Basic Books, 1985.

———. *In God's Shadow: Politics in the Hebrew Bible*. New Haven CT: Yale University Press, 2012.

Wellhausen, Julius. *Prolegomena to the History of Israel*. Atlanta GA: Scholars Press, 1994.

IN THE JPS ESSENTIAL JUDAISM SERIES

Thinking about God: Jewish Views
Rabbi Kari H. Tuling

Thinking about the Prophets: A Philosopher Reads the Bible
Kenneth Seeskin

Thinking about the Torah: A Philosopher Reads the Bible
Kenneth Seeskin

Justice for All: How the Jewish Bible Revolutionized Ethics
Jeremiah Unterman

To order or obtain more information on these or other
Jewish Publication Society titles, visit jps.org.

OTHER WORKS BY KENNETH SEESKIN

Thinking about the Torah: A Philosopher Reads the Bible

Jewish Messianic Thoughts in an Age of Despair

Cambridge Guide to Jewish History, Culture, and Religion (coeditor)

Cambridge Companion to Maimonides (editor)

Maimonides on the Origin of the World

Searching for a Distant God: The Legacy of Maimonides

Maimonides: A Guide for Today's Perplexed